Carson City Century

Nevada's Capital
1900-1999

STEPHEN H. PROVOST

All material © 2022 Stephen H. Provost

Cover concept and design: Stephen H. Provost

All historical photos are in the public domain unless otherwise noted. No part of this book may be reproduced, or stored in a retrieval system, or transmitted in any form or by any means, electronic, mechanical, photocopying, recording, or otherwise, without the express written permission of the publisher.

Century Cities Publishing 2022
A division of Dragon Crown Books
Martinsville, Virginia ♦ Fresno, California
Carson City, Nevada ♦ San Luis Obispo, California
All rights reserved

ISBN-13: 978-1-949971-30-9

Century Cities

Century Cities Publishing was created to celebrate and preserve the history of midsized and smaller American cities during the 20th century. Narratives are presented in timeline form, drawing on major milestones and lesser-known stories from 1900 to 1999. From athletic champions to retail milestones, from city leaders to entertainers, these books provide a panoramic overview of vibrant, growing cities as they came into their own.

Books in this series

Cambria Century, 2021
Carson City Century, 2022
Charleston Century, 2021
Danville Century, 2021
Fresno Century, 2021
Goldfield Century, 2021
Greensboro Century, 2022
Huntington Century, 2021
Roanoke Century, 2021
San Luis Obispo Century, 2021

STEPHEN H. PROVOST

Acknowledgments

Thanks to Scott Schrantz and the University of Nevada-Reno for permission to use their historical photos in the present work. Specific thanks to UNR's manuscripts and archives librarian, Jacquelyn K. Sundstrand and digital access archivist Laura E. Rocke. Special thanks to Sharon Stora for her research and editing assistance.

Contents

1	1900-1909: 'Carson Is Booming'	9
2	1910-1919: Hold Your Horses	29
3	1920-1929: Old West, New World	47
4	1930-1939: Rolling the Dice	57
5	1940-1949: Off the Rails	77
6	1950-1959: Upping the Ante	95
7	1960-1969: Growing Capital	115
8	1970-1979: The Wages of Sin	133
9	1980-1989: Crazy Eighties	167
10	1990-1999: Play On	177

"Towns change; they grow or diminish, but hometowns remain as we left them."

Jayne Anne Phillips,
Novelist

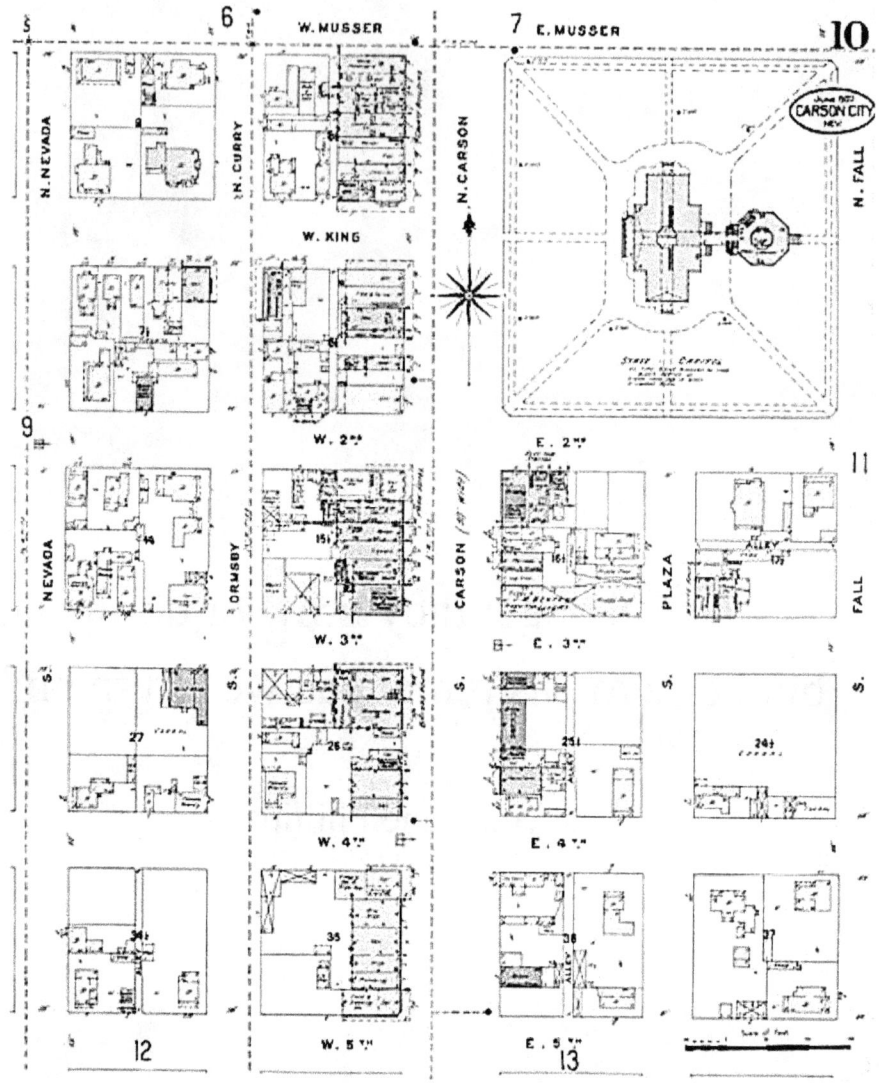

Sanborn Fire Insurance map of downtown Carson City area, centered on Carson Street with the State Capitol in the upper right-hand corner, 1907. *Library of Congress*

Mural in downtown Carson City, 2022. *Author photo*

Introduction

Carson City entered the 20th century as a small town with plenty of tradition to build upon.

The city was named for the Carson River, a name chosen by John C. Frémont to honor Kit Carson, the scout who'd led his 1843 expedition to explore the West. Their trek had taken them as far north as Oregon and west to California, with stops at Lake Tahoe and the areas around what would become Virginia City and Minden.

But Carson City itself wasn't founded until Ohio businessman Abe Curry arrived with a party that included some men he'd met in Utah: among them, attorneys Frank Proctor and John Musser. All three names are familiar to Carson City residents today on streets running through the downtown area.

It was Proctor who named the city, but the party almost didn't get there. They intended to settle in Genoa, Nevada's first town, but Curry's offer of $1,000 for a lot where he'd hoped to build a store was rejected, so they were forced to look elsewhere.

That "elsewhere" turned out to be Eagle Valley, where a post office was established at Carson City in 1858. Considering Curry's attempt to set up a general store in Genoa had been rebuffed, it's ironic that the mayor of Genoa, William Ormsby, wound up establishing the first such store in Carson. He also built a two-story hotel bearing his name that would survive some seven decades.

Warm Springs Hotel c. 1866. *Library of Congress*

Curry, meanwhile, built a hotel of his own in 1861 at the local springs: the Warm Springs Hotel. Nevada State Prison would be built a stone's throw away on land Curry sold to the state for $80,000. As a reward, Curry would be named the prison's first warden. Evidently, the guests at his hotel didn't mind being so close to the lockup.

By then, the town was booming, with hundreds of miners, adventurers, and fortune-seekers passing through following the discovery of silver (the Comstock Lode, named for miner Henry Comstock) near Virginia City. Among them was one Samuel Clemens, aka Mark Twain, who worked as a reporter for the

Territorial Enterprise newspaper in Virginia City, making $25 a week starting in 1862.

Although he worked for the Virginia City paper, Clemens lived mostly in Carson. His older brother, Orion, served as first secretary of the Nevada Territory and built a house there in 1862 at 502 North Division Street. It was in Carson City that the younger Clemens first used the name Mark Twain, which he affixed to one of the news reports he filed in the form of a letter.

Orion Clemens' house in 2022. *Author photo*

Twain would leave the area for San Francisco in 1864, the same year Carson City became the capital of Nevada.

Curry, however, stuck around, even after excitement over the initial silver strike faded and the first lode from 1859 at Comstock started to peter out. He and men like bankers Darius Ogden Mills and William Sharon correctly guessed that there was more ore to be discovered around Virginia City, and timber would be needed to build mines that bored deeper into the earth. In the meantime, miners needed a profitable way to get lower-grade ore down the mountain. Wagons were too expensive, but a railroad would work.

Sharon persuaded Mills to build the Virginia & Truckee Railroad, which was chartered by the Nevada Legislature in 1861 and built between Carson City and Virginia City in 1870. A year later, a branch line was built to Reno, where it hooked up with the Southern Pacific.

The Reno line ran along Washington Street through town to the Carson City Depot at Carson Street. Another line, carrying mostly freight traffic, ran along Caroline Street a block farther south.

Nevada legalized boxing in 1897 expressly to host the heavyweight championship fight between challenger Bob Fitzsimmons, left, and the champion, "Gentleman" Jim Corbett. Fitzsimmons won by a knockout in an upset before 4,000 fans in Carson City.

Meanwhile, in Carson City, Curry had finished building the U.S. Mint and was ready for his next (and, it turned out, his last) major construction project: the machine and car shops for the V&T rail yard. They opened in 1874, and Curry threw a gala ball to celebrate on Independence Day.

There was even more reason to celebrate because Irishman John Mackay had hit on the richest mineral discovering in U.S. history: the "Big Bonanza." Beginning in 1873, Mackay's two mines in the area turned out $3 million a month in precious metal for the next three years. Over a 22-year period, they produced a staggering $180 million in silver and gold.

The mines and the railroad set the stage for Carson City to enter the 20th century, where other industries — government-related businesses, hospitality, and (from the 1930s onward) gambling — would supplant mining as the economic engine that made the capital city run.

Carson City has a rich history as a frontier town in the 1800s that even included a world heavyweight championship fight on St. Patrick's Day in 1897. Nevada actually legalized boxing for the express purpose of allowing the fight between champion Jim Corbett and challenger Bob Fitzsimmons to take place.

Neither man was a heavyweight by today's standards, with Corbett weighing 184 pounds and Fitzsimmons a modern super middleweight at 167.

A crowd of 4,000 people watched as the favored Corbett floored Fitzsimmons in the sixth round and appeared in control of the fight until the 14th round, when Fitzsimmons sent the champ to the canvas with a blow to the stomach that knocked the wind out of him for long enough to end the fight.

A film of the bout, running at more than 100 minutes, is considered the world's first feature film. Events such as these dot Carson City's rich history, and it's impossible to chronicle them all. The city continues to celebrate its 19th century frontier heritage and is growing and thriving today in the 2000s. *Carson Century* tells the story of what happened in between.

The Ferris Wheel was designed by George Washington Gale Ferris, who lived in Carson City, at Third and Division streets, during his youth who unveiled the first one at the 1893 World's Columbian Exposition in Chicago. Each of its 36 cars was able to accommodate 60 people. It was intended to be more impressive than the Eiffel Tower.

'Carson Is Booming'
1900-1909

The Carson City Public School as it appeared on a postcard in the first decade of the 20th century. *Author collection*

1900

Community
According to the *Carson City Appeal*, the town of Gardnerville's new main street boasted "two livery stables, a woodworking shop, a boarding house, a tin shop, three general stores, a hall, four saloons, one meat market, a furniture store, a drug and confectionary store, and two hotels."

Milestones
Carson City was shrinking. With 2,100 residents, its population was less than half of what it had been 20 years earlier (4,229).

1901

Students at the Carson Indian Training School. *University of Southern California Libraries and California Historical Society*

Education

Eight students graduated from the first eighth-grade class at the Stewart Indian School.

The school, built in 1890 on 240 acres at the southern end of Carson City, was one of approximately 200 military-style boarding schools established to house students in the Great Basin area that includes Nevada and Utah, along with portions of California, Oregon, Idaho, and Wyoming.

It was, however, the only one created by a state legislature. Nevada lawmakers passed a bill in 1887 issuing bonds for the school if the U.S. government would agree to operate it. (The Stewart school, originally called the Clear Creek Indian Training School and the Carson Indian Training School, was later renamed for Nevada Senator William Stewart, who pushed legislation that allowed the federal government to run the campus.)

Schools like Stewart were designed to assimilate tribal children, who could be taken from their parents without warning or permission. They'd be moved far away from their families to learn English and job skills. But they were also responsible for doing all the work on campus, from making meals to constructing buildings.

Students were often taken from families, some of whom never saw them again, and given anglicized names. One of them, Richard Barrington, was part of the first eighth-grade class. He'd come to Carson City from Truckee with his family to learn more about the school; as he played beside a pond with a group of Washoe children, school superintendent William D.C. Gibson arrived in a wagon and picked him up, enrolling him in the school under the name "Dickey Jack."

After graduating, Barrington would attend Carlisle Indian School in Pennsylvania, later returning to Stewart as a band instructor.

Most of the children who attended Stewart initially belonged to the Paiute, Shoshone, and Washoe nations, although students were eventually accepted from more than 200 tribes across the West. They wore military-style uniforms and spent the first half of the day in class, while the afternoons were taken up with vocational activities such as farming, masonry, metalwork, and carpentry for the boys; the girls studied things like cooking and dressmaking.

"They got you up at 5 in the morning and put your uniform on, and you had to go out in the cold and drill before breakfast," said Winona James, a Washoe girl who attended Stewart in 1910 and 1911.

Assimilation was forced, and students were compelled to speak English. Punishments could be severe: Food might be withheld, or students might be forced to clean the restroom with a toothbrush. One particularly brutal form of punishment was known as the "hot line," in which young students walked past a line of older students, who were ordered to whip them with their belts.

These punishments continued even in later years, when it became more acceptable to retain native cultural traditions.

"For speaking my native language, I was physically beaten," one Paiute student said. "I was jerked around by my hair several times for getting caught... I kept quiet until I learned English."

That was in 1944.

One student in the early 1960s recalled: "They took this yard-long ruler and hit the back of our calves. They called it swatting. The back of my calves were bruised for six months."

Eighth-grade graduating class at Stewart, 1901. Richard Barrington is second from right in the back row.

1903

Photographer Ed Peterson captured this shot of Carson Street (still unpaved) decked out for a visit from President Teddy Roosevelt on May 19, 1903. *UNRS-P0036-1, Special Collections and University Archives Department, University of Nevada, Reno*

Politics

President Theodore Roosevelt stepped off the train from Reno in Carson City and was, according to the *Reno Evening Gazette*, "much pleased with the beauty, extent, and appropriateness of the town decorations."

"From the railroad to the capitol," the newspaper reported, "the avenue was a continuous series of decorated arches, sweeping banners, flags, and patriotic colors."

Governor John Sparks and Carson City Mayor Will Mackey met the president's party at the state line as he arrived from

California, then accompanied him to the city. Roosevelt spoke from a platform erected at the State Capitol, where the portico was encircled with rifles that formed an arch over the desk from which the president delivered his address. Two buffalo heads raised on Sparks's farm were also among the decorations, and a banner above him read, "Nevada Honors the Hero of San Juan."

Some 15,000 people turned out to see the president, who spoke about topics ranging from tree-cutting to irrigation.

"Until recently, Nevada was only thought of as a mineral and stock-raising state," he said. "Much can be done yet in regards to both the mineral exploitation and the raising of stock within the state."

But, he added, "it is probable that irrigated agriculture will come to the front, and when it does, the people will increase with a rapidity and permanence never before known.

"The State of Nevada has led the way not only in the strength of its plea for national aid in irrigation, but also for its willingness to assist in the work."

Roosevelt arrived in Carson City from Reno about 9 a.m., then headed back to Reno for remarks at the Washoe County Courthouse and University of Nevada before returning to the Golden State.

1904

Education

The cornerstone of the Carson City Public School was laid August 8, in ceremonies conducted by the Masonic Grand Lodge of Nevada.

CARSON CITY CENTURY

1905

Government

Governor John Sparks had a hand in designing Nevada's first state flag, alongside Colonel Harry Day.

Set against a background of the same blue color used on the American flag was the state name at the center. Arrayed above and below were 34 gold and silver stars, with two more on either side of the word "NEVADA," identifying it as the 36th state in the union. At the top, in silver, was the word "SILVER," with the word "GOLD" spelled out at the bottom.

Justice

Four men were hanged at the same time for the murder of Jack Welsh.

They'd killed him for $1.25.

That's how much Welsh had been carrying when the four thieves took it from him and tried to push him off a moving train in Humboldt County. Welsh clung to a side ladder, but ex-con John Sevener kicked him in the face and beat him with a revolver. Then 17-year-old Fred Roberts shot him to death.

Sevener and Roberts were convicted in the killing along with ex-con T.F. Gorman and 20-year-old Albert Lindeman, who was tried separately. All four men were hanged at the Nevada State Prison in Carson City on November 17. It was the second execution at the state prison, following the hanging of an inmate named John Hancock on September 5.

Less than a month after the four men were hanged, two men were hanged together at the prison in the only dual hanging ever recorded there. The two men, Joe Ibapah and a man known as Indian Johnny, had been drinking all day when they came upon a one-legged man near the railroad tracks in

Elko County and demanded that he buy them more liquor. When he refused, they slit his throat, put out his eye, and broke his arm.

The body was found under a pile of railroad ties, and the two murderers were hanged at the prison on December 3.

Transportation

The Virginia & Truckee Railroad was reorganized as the V&T Railway Company, which built a new 15.28-mile branch line from Carson City south to Minden.

1906

Men stand outside Carson City Hot Springs in the early 1900s. *UNRS-P0036-1, Special Collections and University Archives Department, University of Nevada, Reno*

Community

"Carson Is Booming," proclaimed a headline in the *Nevada State Journal*, which listed $150,000 in building projects under way in the city as of March 9.

Among them were a $40,000 state Supreme Court and library building, and $35,000 for a new Carson City Health and Pleasure Resort. Described in the press as a "magnificent sanitarium and casino," the hotel and resort was to be opened a couple of miles outside town on the site of the former Shaw's Springs by July 15.

The entrance to Carson Hot Springs in 2022. *Author photo*

(Shaw's Springs, later known as the Carson Hot Springs, had hosted Gentleman Jim Corbett's training camp prior to his ill-fated heavyweight title defense against Bob Fitzsimmons in 1897.)

Other building projects included annexes to the *Carson News* and State Bank and Trust buildings. ...

The Minden Flour Mill building in 2022.
Author photo

The village of Minden began to take shape at the terminus of the Virginia and Truckee Railway, named after Minden, Germany. The German town was near the birthplace of H.F. Dangberg, whose company submitted a plan for the town to Douglas County commissioners in July of 1906.

Business

The Minden Flour Mill was founded as the first new business in the fledgling town south of Carson City. Financed by the region's wealthiest families (the Dangbergs, Dresslers, and Springmeyers), the mill would add four silos in 1908 that could hold as much as 65,000 bushels of grain.

It was built by the Dangberg Land and Livestock Company.

The steel silos rose 45 feet high and stood adjacent to the brick mill building. During its first decade, it was the tallest building in Minden, rising 3½ stories high, and by the 1920s it was producing 100 barrels of flour a day, in addition to such commodities as chicken and cattle feed.

The mill continued to operate until the 1960s, and it ultimately survived to become the only remaining flour mill among five such structures that were built in the Carson Valley between 1854 and 1906.

Education

The new public schoolhouse, built at a cost of $38,000, opened at Musser and Division streets, with primary-grade classes being housed downstairs and high school courses on the second floor.

The assembly hall, furnished with more than 200 fine chair seats, boasted electric lighting and a good-sized stage.

The bell from the old Central School, which had served students at Minnesota and Telegraph streets since 1872, was transferred to the new facility, with the *Daily Appeal* declaring it sounded "just as natural as ever."

The Carson Exchange

CARSON CITY'S LEADING HOTEL

The best meals for the money
                    Nicely Furnished Rooms
Stage leaves the door daily for Lake Tahoe and all other points   **Meals 25 cents**

F. L. O. DeJarlais, Prop

Lodging

The Carson Exchange advertised itself as "Carson City's Leading Hotel," offering "the best meals for the money" at 25 cents apiece and "nicely furnished rooms." Stagecoaches left daily for Lake Tahoe and "all other points," an ad in the *Daily Appeal* proclaimed.

The ad was part of promotional push by new owner F.X. DeJarlis, who had come to the city the previous year. But the hotel on North Carson Street was already something of an institution, having been open since at least the early 1870s opposite the passenger depot.

Albert Montrose ran the hotel in its early years before moving to Bodie, where he was killed in a boiler explosion in 1890.

The hotel operated until at least 1921, when a short announcement in the *Reno Evening Gazette* declared it was "undergoing a thorough renovation, including the exterior." When DeJarlis's widow died in 1932, it was described in the *Nevada State Journal* as "one of the old landmarks of the state capital."

Retail

Kitzmeyer's Drug Store, owned by C.H. Kitzmeyer, offered "new goods, fresh drugs and reliable service at 'The Old Corner,' formerly the Thaxter Drug Store, corner Carson and King streets." Its line of goods included a "complete stock of high-grade perfumes, soaps and druggist sundries."

A newspaper ad assured readers that "telephone orders

receive prompt attention."

The drugstore would become a longtime fixture on Carson Street.

Transportation

The V&T rail line reached Minden.

1907

Carson City's baseball team poses for the camera. *UNRS-P1992-01-67, Special Collections and University Archives Department, University of Nevada, Reno*

Baseball

The Carson City Capitals were one of four charter members in the new Nevada State League, with teams in Carson City, Reno, Goldfield, and Tonopah populating their rosters with teams from the suddenly smaller Pacific Coast League.

A number of PCL players found themselves out of a job when that circuit contracted from six teams to four, and organizers of the Nevada State League knew a good opportunity when they saw it.

The league was the brainchild of a certain John T. Powers, who enthused: "A baseball league for Nevada would be a great advertising feature for the different towns. The Goldfield parties are already interested, and Bert Ulmer, the manager of the club, is now working on Tonopah and Rhyolite."

Powers called a meeting for May in Reno to set up the new league, with teams envisioned in six cities. (Virginia City and Rhyolite, however, didn't wind up in the final mix.) The season was supposed to last from mid-June to mid-September, with each team playing roughly 80 games.

The *Carson City Daily Appeal* was enthusiastic about the city's new ballclub, boasting that "the Carson infield will compare favorably with any in the country excepting teams in the two big leagues, and then the Capital City boys will hold their own with some of the weaker teams of the National (and) American leagues."

The newspaper compared the club's first baseman, a man named Considine, to future Hall of Famer Frank Chance. Shortstop Broadbent was likened to Joe Tinker, and second baseman Lucera was dubbed "the Lajoie of the Sagebrush" after Nap Lajoie, another future Cooperstown inductee. As impressive as they sounded, none of their first names bore mentioning.

Catcher and team captain "Teddy" Baer was reputed to be the most popular man in town.

"Not since the heavyweight battle between Corbett and Fitzsimmons ten years ago have the people been so enthusiastic over a sport as they have been on this present baseball team," the *Daily Appeal* crowed.

Carson City did, in fact, field a strong team, finishing second in the final standings, percentage points behind Goldfield. But neither the team nor the league would survive a full season: Far from the 80 games projected on the season schedule, the most any team played was 13.

The Goldfield Miners stood atop the standings with a 9-5 record when the season was suspended, with Carson City just behind at 7-4-1. The Tonopah Mollycoddles were third at 3-6, while the Reno Mudhens (or Boosters) brought up the rear with a 3-7-1 record.

Reno's final two games, in mid-July, were both losses to Carson City by scores of 7-3 and 13-9 before anemic weekend crowds of 55 and 157, respectively. They turned out to be Carson's last two games, as well. With the season aborted, an 8-8 tie earlier in the season proved to be the difference between first and second place for the Capitals, who suffered three of their four losses against first-place Goldfield.

Unfortunately, it was the end of organized baseball for the state capital: It was the only time Carson City would field a professional baseball team.

1909

Business

The first Farmer's Bank of Carson Valley opened its doors on October 20 in Minden, operating in its first location for nine years before moving to a larger building across the street. It had $700,000 in resources at that time.

The original building, meanwhile, became home to the Minden Post Office from 1919 to 1974.

The Farmer's Bank of Carson Valley was founded in Minden at its original location, which later served as the town post office. *Author photo*

Community

You could lead horses to this water, and they might actually drink. The water in question came from a fountain placed at the center of the intersection where Carson and King streets met. Horses pulling wagons could dip their heads into the fountain for a drink, and there were even smaller granite bowls at the base for dogs to wet their whistle.

The five-ton fountain was donated to the city by the Hermon Lee Ensign National Humane Alliance, a New York-based animal rights group, and dedicated on Labor Day. Carson City wasn't the only place to get a fountain (although it was the only one in Nevada). The Humane Alliance started making them in 1906 and kept donating them for at least the next five years, until they numbered as many as 125.

When the attorney general's office was built, closing off King Street, the fountain was moved to a spot in front of the new structure.

The fountain in front of the attorney general's office was donated by a humane organization to provide water for horses.
Author photo

Government

The Governor's Mansion was completed at 600 North Mountain Street on land all but donated to the state by Mrs. Thomas B. Rickey (she charged $10).

The two-story building, constructed in Classical Revival style with an imposing front portico supported by four Ionic columns, included 23 rooms. It was first occupied in July by Acting Governor Denver Dickerson — whose wife gave birth to a daughter there just two months later.

George A. Ferris, a Reno architect, was contracted to design the home, which was built for less than $23,000. The name Ferris may sound familiar, as it was shared with George Washington Gale Ferris Jr., the man who designed the Ferris Wheel and also happened to have lived in Carson City.

The Governor's Mansion today. *Author photo*

But that Ferris, a civil engineer who created the original Ferris Wheel for the Chicago World's Columbian Exhibition in 1893, passed away three years after his signature feat and is no relation to the designer of the mansion.

(That first Ferris Wheel, by the way, was much larger than those you're likely to see today: It was fitted with 36 cars, each able to hold up to 60 people, making it capable of carrying 2,160 riders at a time.)

The Minden Auto Camp as it appeared in 2003, shortly before it was torn down. *Photo by Scott Schrantz*

Lodging

There weren't many automobiles on the road in Nevada yet, and the town of Minden was just three years old. But that didn't stop a savvy business owner with an eye on the future from constructing the Minden Auto Camp.

Actually, it began as a shed for the much larger livery stable that was built beside it. With cars becoming more common, however, it was converted into a four-unit "auto camp." Similarly, in time, the livery stable itself was transformed into an auto repair business.

Most auto camps in the 1910s and '20s were little more than plots of land, perhaps equipped with running water, where you could pitch a tent for the night or sleep in your car. As time passed, cabins were added, which in turn gave way to auto courts (or motor courts) and, eventually, motels.

Each of the Minden Auto Camp's four rooms had its own

garage, but the rooms themselves were cozy, to say the least. The low-slung wooden building was simply a row of rooms equipped with Flamo Gas; residents were offered "hot-and-cold showers," and the garage featured Standard Oil products.

Remarkably, the auto camp survived nearly a century at the corner of Second Street and Railroad Avenue, although it was in pretty bad shape by the time the end came. Its white paint had largely been worn away, and old cars had been abandoned in its garages along with oil cans, discarded wheels, and at least one badly decaying mattress.

Plaster was peeling away from the walls in some places, and in other, nothing was left of the walls at all: just gaping holes. The structure was finally torn down in 2003.

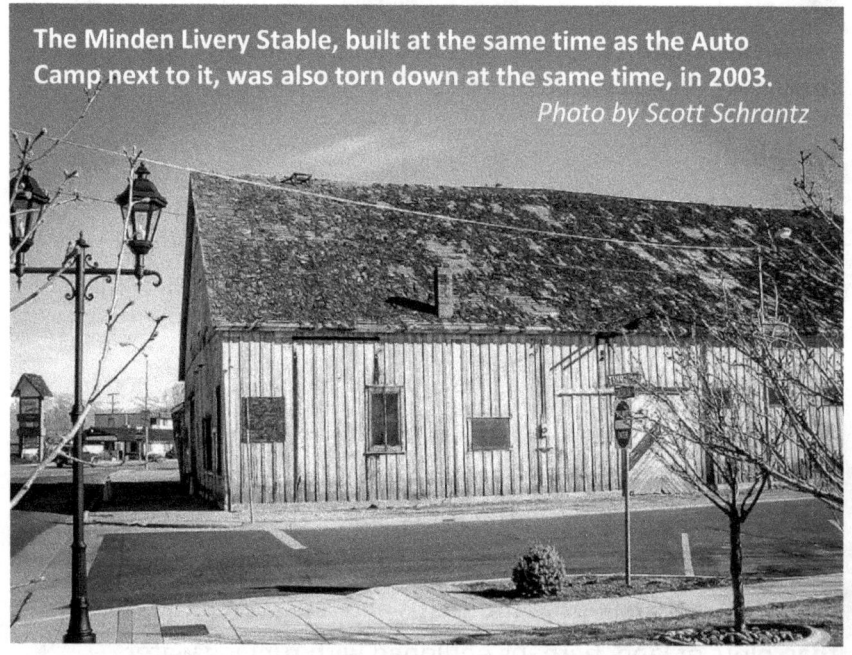

The Minden Livery Stable, built at the same time as the Auto Camp next to it, was also torn down at the same time, in 2003.
Photo by Scott Schrantz

CARSON CITY CENTURY

Hold Your Horses
1910-1919

Carson Street in the teens or twenties. *UNRS-P2006-05-071, Special Collections and University Archives Department, University of Nevada, Reno*

1910

Aviation

It wasn't exactly an airport. It wasn't even a permanent runway. But pilot William Ivy Baldwin made a permanent mark on history as he climbed into the cockpit of the 48-horsepower Paulham biplane he'd had trucked in from Colorado for a landmark flight at Raycraft Ranch north of Carson.

The dirt runway had been cleared away on the occasion of the annual Sagebrush Carnival.

As the crowd watched, the former Army balloonist and veteran of the Spanish-American War rose into the skies above them. It wasn't just the first airplane flight in Carson City history, it was the first ever in the state of Nevada. The biplane traveled a distance of about half a mile, 50 feet above the ground.

Baldwin's flight June 23 was a trial run for an Independence Day exhibition held July 3-5 at Carson City's old horse racing track.

Milestones

Carson City's population had stabilized somewhat at 2,466, having risen 17.4 percent over the previous decade.

Recreation

Clarence Burton purchased Walley Hot Springs for $19,000 in gold coins.

The resort, built by David and Harriet Walley on land they had acquired in 1862, had started out as a small tent bathhouse where baths were offered for 50 cents. Miners from Virginia City frequented the place, allowing it to expand into a $100,000 spa with a 40-room hotel, ballroom, stable, gardens, and 11 baths.

The Walleys' heirs sold the property to John and Richard Raycraft for a mere $5,000, with Jane Raycraft and her husband James Campbell later acquiring it and operating it until 1905. Walley's was touted as offering "amazing remedial energy" for a host of ills at "the most celebrated medicinal spring in Nevada."

Refreshments

Heidelberg Bar opened at Esmeralda and Railroad avenues in downtown Minden. The brick building survived Prohibition, when it served as a soda fountain and grocery store, then reverted to form when it became the Pony Express Saloon in 1941.

By this time, Railroad Avenue was U.S. 395, and the Pony Express took advantage of its prime location to stay in business for some six decades.

The Pony Express eventually took on a new identity as Francisco's Mexican Restaurant.

Francisco's Mexican Restaurant dates back to 1910, when it was founded as a bar in Minden. *Author photo*

The C.O.D. Garage in Minden. *Author photo*

Retail

Minden's Chris Christofferson (no relation to the singer, whose name is spelled differently) opened the town's first dry goods store, also selling clothes, shoes, and cameras. It later became the Town and Country when Tom and Norma Andrews took over management, and the C.O.D. Garage bought the building in 1975, founding Pioneer Motor Parts there.

1911

Basketball

The Douglas County High School basketball team defeated the University of Nevada freshmen 33-31 in what the *Nevada State Journal* described as "one of the hottest and best played basket ball games ever seen here," which the newspaper said featured "a succession of brilliant plays."

Business

Charles Oliver Dangberg broke ground on the C.O.D. garage in Minden. Over the years, it would sell Buicks, Chevrolets, Fords, Hupmobiles, and Jeeps, along with Lauson Tractors, becoming the largest family-owned dealership in Nevada after it was acquired by Fred "Brick" Helwinkel.

In addition to selling vehicles, it also serviced them, providing towing through AAA, selling Goodyear tires, and offering Union Oil and Shell gasoline for sale.

Transportation

Several miles of Carson Street were surfaced, making it the first paved road in the city.

1912

The Carson Valley Improvement Club building in Minden, built in 1912. *Author photo*

Community

The Carson Valley Improvement Club dedicated a new building in Minden, the CVIC Hall. A hub of community activity, it hosted events ranging from movies and theatrical productions to basketball games, weddings, funerals, worship services, political meetings, and even a morgue.

Travel

Motorists arriving at Carson City from California could have their cars serviced at the Raycraft's Garage on North Carson Street, which also sold gas and lubricating oils, or by the Virginia & Truckee Railroad at their shops.

The Raycraft name was prominent in Carson. James Raycraft owned a hotel and a livery stable at Carson and

Musser streets with his brother Joseph. He also bought the Carson Brewing Company in 1900 with partner Frank Golden, and served in the state Assembly from 1908 to 1911. The family ranch was site of Nevada's first airplane flight.

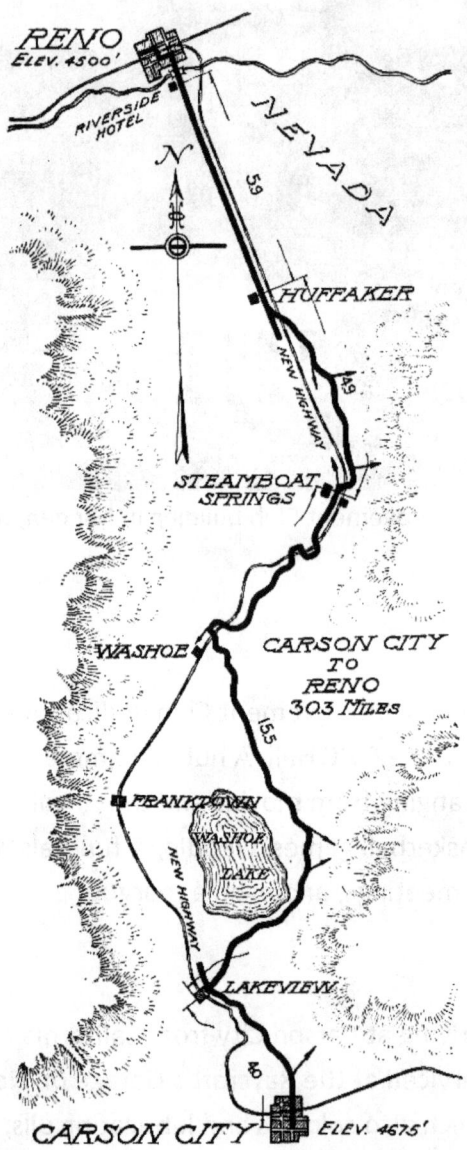

The road between Carson City and Reno, as shown in 1912 California State Automobile Association Tour Book.

Weather

The first week of January saw Washoe Lake frozen over with the heaviest ice in years, but skating wasn't advised because snow was still falling. Carson Lake below Fallon was frozen, too, and skaters were enjoying "plenty of amusement" there, according to a newspaper report.

1913

Justice

A state law passed in 1911 gave prisoners on death row a choice: They could be hanged or face a firing squad.

Andriza Mircovich made his choice.

Mircovich had been found guilty in June 1912 of murdering John Gregovich in Tonopah a month earlier. Gregovich had been the executor for the estate of Mircovich's cousin, and Mircovich was angry about the amount of money he'd been left. He threatened Gregovich, then stabbed him at the Tonopah train station.

Andriza Mircovich was the only prisoner in Nevada ever executed by firing squad.

Mircovich, held at the Nevada State Prison, appealed to the Nevada Supreme Court, but to no avail. When it became clear he was to die, he chose to be killed by firing squad.

But the process hit a snag when warden George Cowing couldn't find five men to serve on the firing squad. According to the *New York Times*, Cowing had "approached a number of men who have absolutely refused to undertake the job of shooting a human being."

The warden urged him to change his mind and choose death by hanging, but Mircovich refused. Cowing therefore placed an order for a 1,000-pound execution machine, but when the "shooting gallery of steel" arrived, Cowing wanted nothing more to do with it and resigned.

The machine worked as planned, and Mircovich was killed instantaneously around midday on May 14, 1913. He was the only prisoner in state history put to death by this method.

Transportation

The first transcontinental road, the Lincoln Highway, was cobbled together out of city streets, rural roads, dirt paths, and anything else that could connect one town to the next.

Named for Abraham Lincoln, the road from New York to San Francisco was the brainchild of Indy 500 speedway builder and Miami Beach developer Carl Fisher, who had made a fortune manufacturing headlights for early cars.

This Lincoln Highway marker stands in front of the Old Mint Building at Carson and Robinson Streets. *Author photo*

West of the Mississippi, the road was rutted, hard to follow, and barely passable in spots. It traversed mile after mile of bleak, unpopulated land — sections of which remain like that to this day. Hence the modern highway's nickname in Nevada, "the loneliest road in America."

Its successor, U.S. Highway 50, follows the route of the old Lincoln Highway west of Ely to a stage stop called Leeteville, near Fallon. There, the Lincoln would split in two, with a northern fork following the path of modern Interstate 80 into Reno along what's called the Donner Route.

The southern fork or Pioneer Route, however, ran along what's now U.S. 50 into Carson City and on from there to the south shore of Lake Tahoe.

The 1924 *Official Road Guide to the Lincoln Highway* pointed out that the southern route, via Carson City, was more direct: "In 1921, the Nevada State Legislature established that branch of the Lincoln Highway running from Fallon to Carson City, by way of Lahontan Dam, as a portion of the state highway system, in line for immediate improvement with state funds and federal aid. ... The southern route is shorter by 14 miles and much more scenic, but does not take you through Reno, the largest city in Nevada."

The guide also described Carson City as being "beautifully laid out," claiming "the distinction of having more shade and fruit trees than any other city in the state."

1914

Lodging

Despite its name, the French Hotel in Gardnerville was actually a Basque Hotel. That's why Peter Borda had a handball court installed at the rear of the hotel in the spring of 1914.

The kind of handball played there was pilota, a traditional Basque game. During the 1930s, teams from as far afield as San Francisco would travel to Gardnerville for championship tournaments. Prize money of $1,000 was at stake in the events: the rough equivalent of $21,000 today.

The French Hotel and Bar in Gardnerville was one of three Basque hotels in town. *Author photo*

The hotel was one of three Basque hotels in Gardnerville during the '30s, and the Borda family operated it for many years. Raymond Borda took the reins after returning from World War II and stayed on as owner for some time.

Despite this stability, the hotel was not without its troubles. In early 1921, the sheriff confiscated seven bottles of jackass brandy, arresting Baptist and Raymond Borda in the process. Both men, however, were freed for lack of evidence a few days later, but the hotel's Prohibition-related struggles weren't over. In April of 1923, it was ordered closed for violating the Volstead Act — only to reopen in October.

1915

Douglas County High School opened in Gardnerville in 1915. The basketball team won a state title the same year.

Basketball

Douglas County High School claimed the state basketball championship by defeating Sparks. The team from Gardnerville, playing on the road, finished the season undefeated in 11 high school games, including a pair of victories over Sparks.

Education

Douglas County High School opened on what is now U.S. Highway 395 in Gardnerville. The school, with its colonnaded portico, was designed by Frederic DeLongchamps, who designed several notable buildings in the area.

The school was converted into a middle school in the 1950s and closed in 1988, but the building is still standing and serves as the Carson Valley Museum & Cultural Center.

Government

Just a decade after adopting its first state flag, Carson City had a new one — this time designed by Carson City schoolteacher and historian Clara Crisler.

The 36 gold and silver stars were retained from the earlier flag but now arrayed in a football shape above and below a central shield. The shield framed a painting highlighting the state's mining, industry, agriculture, railroads, and its location at the base of the Sierra Nevada. It was the same image included on the state seal.

The state motto "ALL FOR OUR COUNTRY" was spelled out on a scroll beneath the shield, which incorporated more than 30 colors, making it expensive to produce. In addition, the scene displayed inside the shield was so complicated it couldn't be sewn but instead had to be painted by hand — not once, but twice (once on each side!).

Despite its popularity, the design would be discontinued in 1929 because of its cost.

1916

Football

The Stewart Indian School sent its football team north for a crucial game against Reno High School.

The game, played in Reno, was a big event: A special train run by the Virginia & Truckee Railroad left Carson at 9:25 in the morning and returned late that Saturday night, giving local fans an opportunity to see the game. The round-trip fare was $1.50.

The Reno team, playing at home, might have hoped for an advantage, but the Stewart squad dominated the game from start to finish, its defense holding Reno scoreless in a 20-0 victory.

The *Carson City Daily Appeal* reported that, "on account of the University team refusing to play the Indians, claiming their season had ended, the championship of the state falls to the Indians."

But the University of Nevada must have had second thoughts, because they ended up playing against Stewart after all.

The result, however, was the same as it had been against Reno High: Stewart won in a shutout, 12-0, leaving no doubt about which team deserved state bragging rights. The *Daily Appeal* related that the Stewart team's "work on the field showed the expert training they had gone through under Prof. McLane, the instructor at the school, and it has made the team the best in the state."

The sports program at the school would be expanded under Superintendent Frederick Snyder in the 1920s, when an Olympic-sized swimming pool was added (it was also used for baptisms), and tennis courts were built. Later students at the school excelled at sports such as cross country and boxing: From 1935 to 1948, Stewart boxers won 10 Nevada Golden Gloves team championships.

Lodging

The 44-room Minden Inn was completed and became a choice stop for celebrities traveling on the V&T Railroad to Minden in the 1930s and '40s.

Designed by Frederic DeLongchamps, who would later

draw up plans for the state Supreme Court and Ormsby County Courthouse buildings in Carson City, it developed a reputation as one of the West Coast's finest small hotels. The Minden Inn operated until 1987, serving drinks and offering gaming to locals and those passing through.

There were four hotels in Carson City in 1916, or you could choose the brand-new Minden Inn a few miles farther south. *Author photo*

Travel

In 1916, travelers who entered Carson City along the Lincoln Highway could spend the night at one of four hotels and have their car serviced at one of four garages.

The Carson Garage in the Carson News Building offered storage and repair services. The garage sold Red Crown Gasoline, oil, air, and auto supplies, "catering especially to the wants of all travelers." Michelin tires and tubes were "always in stock," and the garage included Buick and Mitchell Motor Car service stations.

The speed limit through town was 15 miles per hour, and it was enforced.

1917

Transportation

The July 15, 1921 issue of *Motor West* recalled that one L.E. Gilcrease had driven a Hudson automobile over an unpaved road between Carson City and Reno in 46 minutes in 1917.

The magazine cautioned its readers that "present detours hinder speed, and on the east side of Washoe Lake the road is wretched."

1918

The second Farmer's Bank in Minden opened in 1918 and would survive the Great Depression. *Author photo*

Community

The second Farmer's Bank was built in Minden and would operate downtown for half a century. It was able to survive the Depression when many other banks were not, and was one of the first to reopen after President Franklin Roosevelt declared a bank holiday in 1933.

1919

Education

Dewey Sampson of the Northern Paiute nation, graduated from Stewart Indian School. He would go on to become the first American Indian legislator in Nevada, serving in the Assembly from 1939 to 1940. Sampson also helped write the bylaws and constitution for the Pyramid Lake Paiute Tribe and worked as a Paiute translator.

Transportation

A two-mile-long convoy of military vehicles carrying a group of weary soldiers pulled into Carson City on August 30, nearing the end of a cross-country road trip along the Lincoln Highway.

Lt. Col. Charles McClure led a group of two dozen officers and some 250 enlisted personal that included Capt. Dwight D. Eisenhower. The journey, Eisenhower later reflected, took the line of tanker trucks, field kitchens, ambulances, and other vehicles "through darkest America."

The Lincoln Highway was unpaved over large stretches and barely more than a dirt track (if that) west of the Mississippi. And the road was so poorly marked that scouts on motorcycles were sent ahead to be sure they were still on the right course. Flimsy and barely maintained bridges gave way under the weight of the vehicles, and a towing tractor with a power winch was needed to extricate them from muddy riverbeds.

A military convoy that includes future president Dwight Eisenhower passes through eastern Wyoming en route to Nevada and California on the Lincoln Highway. *National Archives*

The road got so bad through Wyoming and Utah that the convoy used an abandoned Union Pacific right-of-way instead. Eisenhower labeled the Lincoln Highway in Utah nothing more than a "succession of dust, ruts, pits, and holes," where vehicles repeatedly got bogged down in the salt flats.

Things were little improved when the convoy reached Nevada, where a number of vehicles got stuck in sand traveling from Fallon to Carson City. They straggled into Carson City between 4 p.m. and midnight, with the soldiers being treated to a well-deserved Sunday respite at the Carson Hot Springs and tours of prominent community sites like the Governor's Mansion and Stewart Indian School.

Their stay in Carson was short, however, as they resumed their journey west toward Lake Tahoe the following day. ...

State highway officials selected a route east of Washoe lake for the state highway between Carson City and Reno after weighing the costs of construction and the money needed to purchase rights of way.

More county funds were generally expended along the west side of the road, where more farms and residents could be found. However, it was determined that the eastern route would be less expensive to build and would remain open to travel for a much longer period each year.

Old West, New World
1920-1929

Hollywood came to Carson City in the 1920s, with scenes from the film Desperate Trails being filmed at Nevada State Prison.

1920

Cinema

The Rex Theatre opened with 477 seats at 1430 Main Street in Gardnerville.

In addition to the theater area, the building also included two stores, three office suites, and four extra rooms. It was damaged by fire in 1928, but was refurbished and reopened as the Nevada Theater, which remained in business until the 1960s.

Milestones

Carson City's population had fallen again during the 1910s, dipping by nearly one-third to 1,685.

1921

Cinema

Exterior shots of Nevada State Prison were seen in the silent film *Desperate Trails*, directed by John Ford and starring Harry Carey as an innocent convict bent on vengeance against those who'd put him behind bars.

Crime

Halloween hijinks got a little out of hand, the *Carson Daily Appeal* reported. A group of boys and young men tore down fences, ripped several house gates off their hinges and carried them away, and turned horses out into the street. Two residents responded by threatening to "call out the old musket, and the boys will have to call in a doctor to extract the birdshot."

1922

Cinema

The Grand Theater was showing Paramount's *Forbidden Fruit* along with an Aesop's Fables cartoon, a Hal Roach comedy, Pathe News, and William Desmond in *A Broadway Cowboy*. The latter reportedly had "laughs, thrills, suspense, and romance, and action aplenty."

Admission could be had for a quarter or 55 cents.

The Ormsby County Courthouse was completed in 1922, using a design by Frederic DeLongchamps. *Author photo*

Community

The Ormsby County Courthouse, built at a cost of $65,735, was completed in March.

Transportation

A new concrete road was constructed connecting Reno, Carson City, and Minden. Begun in 1921 and completed in '22, the road was laid out parallel to the V&T rail line and was later incorporated into the federal highway system as part of U.S. 395.

The highway proved to be a problem for the V&T, which began operating at a loss the following year as freight shifted from the rails to the new highway and former train passengers began driving instead.

1923

The Stewart Indian School administration building, like many others on campus was a stone structure. *Author photo*

Education

A new 7,000-square-foot stone building, housing the administration and student union, was completed at the Stewart Indian School. In addition to administration offices, it housed a switchboard and stenographer.

The new stone building was just the latest improvement at the school, which had begun a key transformation — from a failing school with rundown buildings into a more attractive learning environment — upon the arrival of new superintendent Frederick Snyder in 1919.

It was Snyder who brought in Hopi stonemasons to construct more than 60 new buildings, using stones from a quarry along the Carson River and teaching the students masonry in the process. He also added landscaping to the school in the form of trees, flowerbeds, and rose trellises that connected the buildings.

Buildings on the Stewart Indian School campus, from top, include the old gym, the 1925 auditorium, and a post office. *Author photos*

Single-story stone cottages were built to replace deteriorating wooden buildings.

Also among these buildings was the new administration building. An Indian Office inspector said Snyder was "very proud of this building, which is really more ornate than useful for the purpose for which it is intended."

Stewart Indian School dining hall. *Author photo*

1924

Justice

Nevada became the first state to execute a prisoner using toxic gas, putting 29-year-old Gee Jon to death for killing Tom Quong Kee in a "tong war" between Chinese underworld groups.

Jon was executed in a stone building lined with steel in the prison yard that had been built for the purpose. He was strapped to a pine chair, and hydrocyanic gas was sprayed into the 10-by-12 chamber. He was dead within six minutes.

1926

The Minden Mercantile opened in 1926 and added a drugstore in 1931. *Author photo*

Retail

Two Williams, Heitman and Rood, opened Minden Mercantile, selling groceries, farm supplies, and hardware in downtown Minden. Five years later, C.B. Braden opened a drugstore inside the building.

John Ellis expanded the array of merchandise for sale in 1939, adding toys, confections, and electrical supplies. He also lured customers with options of home delivery and charge-account purchases.

Transportation

The U.S. federal highway system, with its black-lettering on white shields, was formed. As part of the system, U.S. Highway 395 was designated, but it didn't run through Carson City (or anywhere close) just yet. In fact, the numbering at this point only applied to a section of road between Spokane, Washington, and the Canadian border.

1927

Aviation

Charles Lindbergh flew from Reno to Carson City, Yosemite, and Death Valley.

1928

The Carson City Airport, seen in 2022, was founded in 1928. *Author photo*

Aviation

Three local families offered a 76-acre site on which to establish the Carson City Airport. The airport would be expanded in the 1940s and '50s to accommodate an east-west runway that took advantage of westerly Sierra Nevada winds.

The public airport, three miles northeast of downtown, would eventually grow into the third-busiest general aviation airport in Nevada, featuring a 75-foot-wide, 6,100-foot-long runway.

Justice

Inmates at Nevada State Prison began making license plates. From that time until the prison closed, all license plates issued in the state were manufactured by inmates there.

Lodging

The Travelers Hotel had already been through a couple of name changes by the time 1928 rolled around. It had been built way back in 1862 as the St. Charles and served as a stagecoach stop, housing offices of the Pioneer Stage Company. The three-story hotel stood adjacent to a two-story inn called the Muller that was completed shortly afterward.

The St. Charles became the Briggs Hotel in 1890 and was combined with the Muller four years later to become the Briggs House. Then, in 1910, the name changed again, this time to the Golden West, a far less fashionable stop where the owner paid local boys a quarter a head to catch jackrabbits that could be served for dinner in the evening.

As the Travelers, it had a bar and café on the first floor, and the second-floor balcony had been removed.

After World War II, the name would change again to the Hotel Page, touted as a hotel and casino with a steak house and cocktail lounge on the bottom floor. A coat of white plaster covered the original brick as the hotel took on the kind of Art Deco motif popular at the time; it also served as a Greyhound Bus depot.

The Page lasted less than a decade before the name was changed yet again, in 1953, to the Pony Express Hotel, which also housed the Mite As Well Bar.

1929

Government

The design for Nevada's state flag was adopted on March 26. A cobalt blue background made up most of the flag; in the upper left corner, a five-pointed silver star was set between two crossed branches of sagebrush (the state flower) and beneath yellow-gold scroll inscribed with the words "BATTLE BORN," written in black.

The gold letters N, E, V, A, D, and A were arrayed around the star, a design that would be altered slightly in 1991 to spell out "NEVADA" underneath the star.

CARSON CITY CENTURY

Rolling the Dice
1930-1939

The Arlington Hotel on Carson Street had been standing for more than half a century by the time the 1930s rolled around. It took up most of the block between Spear and Robinson. This photo shows it sometime between 1925 and 1935. *UNRS-P2006-05-063, Special Collections and University Archives Department, University of Nevada, Reno*

1930

Milestones

The population in Carson City dipped for the fourth time in five decades, bottoming out at 1,596 for the 1930 census.

1931

Divorce

When people think about changes in the law that shifted the course of Nevada's future, they often think of the state's decision to legalize gambling.

That happened this year too.

But while gaming took a while to become a big moneymaker for the state, Nevada's decision to reduce the waiting period for divorce reaped immediate dividends. With the Depression in full swing, the state was strapped for money, especially with the mining industry in places like Goldfield and Tonopah all but tapped out.

Despite moral objections, money was a larger consideration. Nevada had already found that it could make money by reducing its residency requirement for divorce. In 1927, it had cut the waiting period to three months. (Banking magnate George Wingfield had supposedly pushed for the bill to create business for his new Riverside Hotel in Reno, where the concept had support from the mayor and others.)

The change from the previous six-month waiting period produced immediate dividends, with the number of divorces jumping from 1,000 to 2,500 in a single year. In 1930, a total of 3,000 were granted in Reno alone, producing $3 million in revenue for the state.

Nearby states, meanwhile, were taking notice, with Arizona, Idaho, Montana, New Mexico, and Wyoming all considering 90-day residency rules. Nevada, however, stayed one step ahead of them by introducing a bill that specified a seven-week waiting period. The period was shortened to six weeks in committee, prompting Humboldt County Senator Duane Bush to quip that the state might as well legalize "mail-order divorce" to ensure no other states shortened the period further.

Some opponents worried that the law would attract temporary residents and transients. Rural counties, meanwhile, saw it as a boon to Reno. They said they'd only back the bill if new residents were allowed to live wherever they wanted and even travel around within the state, rather than requiring that they file in the county where they lived — a requirement under the previous law.

Another amendment specified that divorce hearings be closed and transcripts be sealed. The move was designed to encourage well-known and wealthy individuals to file for divorce in the state by ensuring their privacy was protected.

Governor Fred Balzar signed the bill into law on March 19, and 1931 saw the state grant 5,260 divorces, with 90 percent of them being in Reno. Divorces generated between $1 million and $5 million a year for the state during the thirties. And by 1981, Nevada's divorce rate was 10 times the national average, but people were getting married there too: 10 times as many as in the state with the next-highest figure, South Carolina.

Education

Future governor Paul Laxalt was already distinguishing himself, making the third-grade honor roll at the Carson City elementary school.

Fire

A malfunctioning furnace ignited an April 4 blaze that destroyed the old Carson Opera House at 507 West Spear Street. Built in 1878 with a room for 790 theatergoers, it had welcomed minstrel shows, political speakers, opera companies, plays, and vaudeville performers.

Standing next to the Excelsior Hotel, it was equipped with a wood stove that could also burn coal, which filled the place with sooty smoke.

Patrons didn't care, but it was certainly a fire hazard, so a new furnace was installed — and it was that furnace that malfunctioned, igniting the fire that literally brought down the house.

The Carson Opera House burned in 1931. *Elmorovivo, cinematreasures, Creative Commons 2.0*

By the time the blaze broke out that destroyed it, the old opera house had been operating as the Grand Theatre, showing movies, since 1913.

Today, the Carson Nugget casino sits where the venerable old theater once stood.

Carson Street in the 1930s. *University of Southern California Libraries and California Historical Society*

Gaming

It wasn't that Nevada didn't have gambling in 1931. It had plenty of it. But money wasn't going to the state — which really needed it at that point — but to crooked cops and officials on the take.

The argument for legalizing games of chance was the same one used over the years for legalizing prostitution, state lotteries, and marijuana dispensaries: If it was happening anyway, the state might as well get a cut.

Ironically, those who wanted gambling legalized weren't above using the same methods they'd used when it was illegal: bribes and payoffs. When Los Angeles cracked down on illicit gaming, major players there such as Tony Cornero, John Grayson, and Guy McAfee set their sights on the virgin territory of Las Vegas.

They sent representatives like Murray Humphreys, John Roselli, and the father-son team of Frank and John Detra to pave the way for legalized gambling in Nevada. They did so by greasing the palms of state lawmakers. Journalist Guy Russo recalled that the Detras delivered briefcases stuffed with cash to movers and shakers across Nevada to enlist their support for the so-called Wide Open Gambling Bill.

Gambler Jimmy "the Crab" Welsh told the Reno Chamber of Commerce in early 1931 that gaming would go on in the city whether it was legal or not: "You can't stop it."

"Reno is known now as a wide-open town," he said, "and there is no reason why gambling should not be thrown wide-open and a Monte Carlo established here. It would mean additional revenue for the city.

"Gambling cannot be stopped here or anywhere else. It's just like Prohibition. Is there anyone here who is brainless enough to say that I can't get a drink in any town in the United

States today? And the Prohibition law is supposedly universal in this country."

It wasn't the first time legalized gambling had been proposed in Nevada. In 1925, another wide-open gambling bill had been introduced but had been defeated in the state Assembly on a vote of 22-13. The idea had resurfaced, and a bill supporting it had passed the Assembly two years later, only to be defeated in the state Senate on a 9-8 vote.

Things were looking different, though, when Assemblyman Phil Tobin of Humboldt County introduced a new bill on February 13, 1931.

"I was just plumb sick and tired of seeing gambling going on all over the state and payoffs being made everywhere," Tobin said. "Some of these tinhorn cops were collecting 50 bucks a month for allowing it. Also, the damn state was broke, and we needed the money."

Not everyone was in favor of the idea, even among gamblers. Stuart Curtis, financial analyst for the state's Gaming Control Board, wrote that Tonopah gamblers said they'd rather keep running games under cover, because they thought many of their patrons would balk at the prospect of being seen patronizing open gaming.

Despite such misgivings, the bill passed March 17, a day after the six-week divorce bill cleared the legislature, and both were signed on the same day March 19 by Governor Fred Balzer.

Reno Mayor E.E. Roberts said the change was long overdue, remarking, "Now we can do lawfully what Nevada has always done under cover."

While most of the action went to Reno and Las Vegas, Carson City would wind up with some casinos of its own before long.

1932

George Wingfield

Business

Even the influx of money from quickie divorces and legalized gambling couldn't save the state from major fallout during the Depression. Banks were especially hard hit, and Governor Fred Balzar was forced to declare a two-week bank holiday beginning November 1 to avoid a run on the banks.

Some financial institutions were too far gone to survive. Foremost among them were a dozen banks owned by tycoon George Wingfield, who'd made his money initially from the mining boom in Goldfield just after the turn of the century.

Wingfield's banks held nearly two-thirds of the deposits in the entire state, but they were all forced to close, including the Carson Valley Bank. Wingfield himself filed for bankruptcy.

Prison

The legalization of gambling in Nevada didn't just affect law-abiding citizens. Inmates at Nevada State Prison got into the act, too.

After gambling became legal, correctional officers decided it would be a good way to keep inmates occupied, so they set up blackjack, poker, and craps tables in the prison dining hall. Sports betting was also allowed. Later, the casino was housed in a room just off the prison yard, through a short door and down a long, stone hallway.

As many as 100 inmates could gamble at once in what was known as the "Bullpen," the only prison gambling hall in the country.

Brass coins that were used as currency for food or laundry at the prison were wagered at the gambling tables, which were run by the inmates themselves. Denominations ranged from a nickel to $5, and there was even a cashier's cage. The prisoners were afraid the games might be shut down if cheating was discovered, so it wasn't tolerated. A percentage of the take went to an inmate welfare fund.

"These guys are experts," warden Art Bernard said in 1957, referring to the inmates who ran the casino. "You can be sure they allow no cheating whatever."

View of the Nevada State Prison when it was operating. *University of Southern California. Libraries and California Historical Society*

Inmates who gambled at the Bullpen included Joe Conforte, owner of the Starlight Ranch in Mound House and the more famous Mustang Ranch, who was photographed playing craps there in the early 1960s. Conforte even ran some of the games when he was an inmate in 1962, adding horse racing and college athletics to the list of things inmates could wager on.

Nevada State Prison, now closed, is seen in 2022. Like other places in Nevada, it had its own casino, run by the inmates. *Author photo*

The Bullpen continued to operate until 1967. One legislator, Howard McKissick of Reno, even justified it by arguing that gambling prevented "homosexual problems."

But there was a riot at the prison that year, and several lawmakers got behind a bill to shut down the casino. It didn't pass, but new warden Carl Hocker closed the Bullpen after deciding that activities such as bridge, chess, table tennis, shuffleboard, and crafting would be better distractions for inmates.

"I think gambling in prison is a degradation, and it's certainly not constructive," he said. "We're trying to replace it with constructive, wholesome activities that will contribute to a decent, healthful state of mind."

Scenes at Nevada State Prison after its closure include guard tower and execution chamber, left, in top photo; a cell meant to house two inmates, at left; and a door to the prison, above. *Author photos*

1933

The first Carson Theatre opened in 1933. Today, the building houses a coin dealer. *Author photo*

Cinema

The first of two movie houses to bear the name Carson Theatre opened in a building that dated from the turn of the century and had once housed the Old Sagebrush Club.

The former men's club was refurbished and opened in 1933 as a 400-seat Art Deco cinema. The Christmas feature that year was Ed Wynn in *The Chief*, showing at 6, 8, and 10 p.m.

The cinema would continue operating for the next couple of decades at 603 North Carson Street.

1934

The Stewart Indian School "S" is still visible today. *Author photo*

Education

Change was in the air at the Stewart Indian School. Alida Bowler, the first female superintendent of the Bureau of Indian Affairs, shifted the emphasis away from assimilation and toward a curriculum that focused on tribal heritage in the form of traditional crafts, songs, dances, and art.

Another milestone for the school took place in 1934, as students climbed a hillside east of town and painted a large letter "S" overlooking the school.

The letter remains visible today.

Transportation

The federal government designated various state highways as part of U.S. 395, which it extended all the way to San Diego. Among the Nevada state routes incorporated into the federal highway was Nevada Route 3 (the "Bonanza Highway"), which ran through Gardnerville and Minden to Carson City and onward to Reno.

U.S. 395 shields, Minden. Author photo

U.S. 395 shields were placed along the route in Nevada the following year.

1935

Fire

The wooden hotel at Walley's Hot Springs burned down.

1936

Dining

An ad for the New Year's Eve grand opening of Hunter's Lodge in Carson City touted the new establishment as the "most unique Cocktail Room in Nevada." A special New Year's Eve dinner would be served for 75 cents from 1 to 9 p.m., with patrons dining to music from a live orchestra.

The Minden Inn was planning a New Year's Eve dance, as well, with "noise makers" and "good music."

Education

A group of seniors at Stewart Indian School founded the Wa-Pai-Shone Craftsmen Inc., a cooperative and trading post that was created under Nevada law.

The trading post at Stewart was the group's base of operations, and it ultimately expanded to include other posts in Death Valley, at Bishop, and at Crystal Bay — a hub for some early casinos along the north shore of Lake Tahoe.

Transportation

The paint shop at the V&T Railroad shops was closed following the death of Joseph Castle, who'd been painting V&T cars and locomotives for 46 years.

1937

Government

The state's Supreme Court had a new home: a 21,000-square-foot Art Deco building that also housed the state library and offices for the attorney general.

Built at a cost of $160,000, it was constructed between the Ormsby County Courthouse and Heroes Memorial Building, with the same architect who had designed both — Frederic DeLongchamps — once again doing the honors.

Tennis

Paul Laxalt would later distinguish himself in court as an attorney, but in 1937, he stood out on a different kind of court: the tennis court. Laxalt captured the Nevada junior tennis title and also defeated Sacramento's tennis champion in convincing fashion, 6-1, 6-3.

1938

Basketball

Carson High defeated Stewart for the state championship in a low-scoring affair, 22-12.

Actor Pat Morita ("Happy Days," "The Karate Kid"), rides as grand marshal in the 2004 Nevada Day Parade. *Photo by Scott Schrantz*

Community

Most kids around the country would love to have Halloween as a day off. In Nevada, they did.

October 31 just happens to be the day Nevada was admitted to the union back in 1864 — which was made a discretionary state holiday in 1933 with the passage of a bill introduced by Carson City Senator Ira Winters.

But Carson City (along with Douglas, Lyon, and Storey counties) celebrated Halloween the day before in order to avoid a conflict. At least that meant older kids could stay out later trick-or-treating, if their parents allowed it.

In 2000, the legislature would move the Nevada Day celebration to the Friday before October 31.

The tradition of a Nevada Day celebration (then more commonly known as Admission Day) started out in Reno, but interest had begun to flag there by 1937, so Carson City Judge Clark Guild and Thomas C. Wilson, a journalist who would start Reno's first ad agency a year later, took matters in to their own hands. (Wilson's signature ad campaign was his "Harold's Club or Bust" promotion in Reno.) With the help of the Carson City Rotary, Lions Club, and 20-30 Club, the two men got the Nevada Day celebrations moved to Carson City.

A special 10-car train carrying 750 visitors pulled in from Reno on the V&T Railroad just in time for the morning parade, which featured the Carson City Band and eight other bands, along with floats and a high-wheel bicyclist, among others.

The Reno High School band beat out the Stewart Indian School contingent as the top band, according to the judges.

The United Spanish American War Veterans of Reno entered a float with an old-time medicine show theme, advertising "The Tiger Fat Medicine Company" and adorned with a papier-mâché tiger. The Eagles Lodge, meanwhile, entered a "saloon on wheels." But top honors went to the Carson Lions Club for its historic float.

Alex McCharles of Carson City was deemed to have the best costume, portraying Abraham Lincoln, while second and third prizes went to individuals dressed up as Kit Carson and John C. Fremont.

There was a historical pageant, Civil War-era costume

ball, and a "Pony Express" race from Virginia City to Carson City. The event was a huge success, with more than 19,000 people turning out.

More than 1,000 people attended the pageant alone, which featured participants in costumes of Native Americans, Civil War soldiers, and (of course) Kit Carson, among others. All 1,000 of them joined together in singing the "Sagebrush Hymn" at the pageant's finale. Fireworks after dark near the high school concluded the festivities.

The annual celebration has been held in Carson City every year since, except for three years during World War II.

Refreshments

Broderick's Old Corner Bar and Cocktail Lounge opposite the Arlington Hotel invited visitors to "make it a point of pleasure — to have a refreshment visit with us whenever you're in the capital. We serve the best."

Tennis

More than 500 fans turned out to watch Paul Laxalt take the court against defending high school boys' champion Verne Brown of Reno. The occasion: a dedication ceremony for Carson City's new high school courts.

Laxalt, described in the press as the protégé of former Olympic, Wimbledon, and U.S. Open champion Helen Wills Moody, came through like a charm, defeating Brown 6-2, 6-4.

It was a big year for Laxalt, who also played on the state champion boys' basketball team.

Transportation

The foundry at the V&T Railroad shops was closed, and the railroad went into federal receivership. Stockholder Ogden

Mills had loaned the railroad $95,000 of his own money over the previous six years to help it balance the books, but his death put an end to that stream of revenue.

By 1937, the V&T had been forced to start selling assets to pay the bills.

The railroad operated at a net income deficit of more than $440,000 from 1928 to 1947.

A view of the V&T Railroad Shops in 1972. *Historic American Buildings Survey, Library of Congress*

1939

Community

Work was completed on the Civic Auditorium, a red-brick building at 813 North Carson Street, designed by Lehman A. Ferris, a Reno architect whose father had drawn up plans for the Governor's Mansion. (Lehman Ferris was also Nevada's first building inspector.)

The auditorium was designed to serve a variety of

purposes, hosting events as diverse as dances, stage plays, public meetings, and basketball games. Later, it housed the first Ormsby County Library. ...

The former Carson City Civic Auditorium. *Author photo*

Attendance more than doubled for the second Nevada Day celebration held in Carson City, which had expanded to three days and welcomed 45,000 participants and spectators. This year's event marked the 75th anniversary of Nevada's statehood.

Off the Rails
1940-1949

The Carson City Depot in 1940. *Arthur Rothstein, Library of Congress*

1940

Cinema

Roy Rogers played the title character in *The Carson City Kid*, A Republic Pictures release that ran just under an hour. Rogers portrayed a character whose given name was Roy Rogers, but he wasn't playing himself. And although the film's title refers to Carson City, it wasn't filmed there (but rather, in Chatsworth, California).

Customers congregate at the bar inside the Carson Brewery in 1940. Note the woodstove in the background of the bottom photo. *Arthur Rothstein, Library of Congress*

Milestones

Carson City reversed its previous trend by adding to its population. It still was far from a metropolis, but 55.3 percent growth brought the number of residents to 2,478.

1941

Citation

Actress Ava Gardner was on the hook for $15, which she paid to settle a speeding ticket in Carson City. Gardner was poised to marry Frank Sinatra, who was getting a divorce in Nevada.

Politics

C.B. Austin became the first person elected mayor of Carson City, with voters handing him a two-year term. World War II, however, forced the cancellation of the next scheduled vote, in 1943, so Austin wound up serving four years instead.

Transportation

The V&T rail lines between Virginia City and Carson City were pulled up and sold for scrap, and the profit from those sales helped keep the railroad operating.

1942

Cinema

William Holden starred in *The Remarkable Andrew*, a comedy involving the ghost of Andrew Jackson that was filmed in the Old Federal Building (Laxalt Building), the Rinckel House at 102 Curry Street, and other locations around Carson City.

The Senator Cafe is seen in this 1949 photo of the Kit Carson Post Rifle Squad participating in the "Gratitude Train Parade." *UNRS-P2007-11-1, Special Collections and University Archives Department, University of Nevada, Reno*

Dining

The Senator Café was operating at Carson and Musser streets downtown, across from the courthouse.

The café, not to be confused with the Senator Bar down the street, was open all night and served up everything from trout and oysters to steaks and filets (all less than $2) in the 1940s. A full Chinese dinner for two was $4.

For breakfast, you could order liver and bacon for $1.10; a cream waffle or little thin dollar cakes for 35 cents each; and peaches, apricots, or figs for a quarter apiece. Doughnuts were 15 cents for two, and Grapenuts, Corn Flakes, or Rice Krispies were 30 cents each (all served with pure cream).

You could get sandwiches, potatoes, burgers, or veggies for lunch. Grilled cheese would cost you a quarter, and if you had another quarter, you could add ham to that. There were pies, shakes, and sundaes for dessert, and a full bar serving wine, beer, and cocktails.

Baseball great Ty Cobb apparently visited the place, or at least signed one of its matchbooks.

1943

Military

Carson Mayor C.B. Austin smashed a bottle of champagne against the bow of a new 303-foot Navy patrol frigate at the Port of Los Angeles. And with that, the ship was christened the USS Carson City.

It was the 50th of more than 100 ships in its class to be named for small and middle-sized U.S. cities between 1942 and 1944.

The USS Carson City took part in landings on Morotai Island, west of New Guinea, where it was assigned to conduct patrol duties and escort U.S. supply ships. During the landings on Morotai, for which the ship earned a Navy Battle Star, its crew fired at Japanese aircraft (though none were hit).

Later, it also took part in landings at Leyte, an island in the Philippines, earning a second Battle Star for its role there.

In an encounter with a Japanese submarine during its patrols, the Carson City dropped depth charges on the enemy ship, though it isn't known whether the sub was damaged.

After the war, the Carson City was sent north for patrol duties off Alaska, then later put on loan to the Soviet and, later, the Japanese navies. It was sold in 1971 to a company in Taiwan, which wrecked it for scrap metal.

V&T Railroad shops, looking east, photographed in 1972. *Historic American Buildings Survey, Library of Congress*

Transportation

The machine shop at the V&T Railroad shops was closed, with more than 35 percent of the equipment being sold — much of it for scrap to bolster the war effort.

1944

Justice

Floyd Loveless, 17, became the youngest person ever put to death at Nevada State Prison after being condemned for the shooting murder of a constable when Loveless was just 15 years old.

1945

Basketball

Earl Dunn became the first player in Nevada history to score at least 40 points in a game, pouring in 42 in Stewart

Indian School's 64-29 win over Fallon. He later added a 40-point showing against Yerington, as Stewart rolled to an 84-25 win.

By the time the season was about to wrap up, Dunn had scored 327 points with two games left, almost twice as many as the second-best scorer in the Western Nevada League.

The fact that Dunn played center but stood just 5-foot-10 made his exploits all the more impressive.

The following season, Dunn scored 29 points against Reno High, considered the top team in northern Nevada, outscoring the Huskies all by himself as Stewart romped 49-28. His exploits that January night led Reno High coach Herb Foster to label his effort "the greatest individual performance I have ever seen by a high school player."

Just five days later, Dunn outscored the entire Sparks team, racking up 28 points to his opponents' 24. Then, on February 1, he broke his own state record with 46 points in a 69-35 demolition of Fallon. As of 2020, it was still the ninth-best total all-time in Nevada's Division 1A.

Dunn earned first-team all-state honors in 1946 after being a second-team choice a year earlier. He also excelled as a wide receiver in football, where he earned all-state honors and was labeled a "pass-catching wizard" in the press.

He competed as a pitcher in baseball, and as a boxer, he advanced to the finals of the 1944 Golden Gloves AAU tournament.

Gaming

The Golden Bubble Casino opened in Gardnerville at 1440 U.S. Highway 395.

It would later become Sharkey's Casino.

Politics

George Lind, who had represented the city's Third Ward since 1941, became mayor; he would serve until 1947.

1946

This V&T passenger car was converted into a diner for a time. *Author photo*

Transportation

The V&T Railroad shops were officially closed. The foundry would be rented privately two years later.

Car No. 22 from the railroad, a McKeen Motor Car, had been retired a year earlier but would soon be converted to serve a different purpose: In August of 1946, it became a Denny's Diner.

No, it's not the same well-known chain that exists today (and includes a location in Carson City). Those eateries, originally known as Danny's Donuts, didn't come along until the early '50s. This one was named for its owner, Alva Dennison.

McKeen had produced 152 of its motor cars, equipped with internal-combustion engines that were cheaper to run on commuter rail lines. V&T purchased this particular one in 1910.

Its size, stretching all the way out to 70 feet, and large porthole-style windows made it well-suited to its new role as a diner. Tables lined both sides of the rail car, and there was an eight-seat counter, along with a couple of slot machines — which, unfortunately, were stolen around the beginning of 1947. The thieves made off with $120 in nickels and dimes, and the machines themselves were found, wrecked and discarded, by a highway crew in Washoe Valley.

Inside the restored V&T passenger car. *Author photo*

The diner had a prime location at Carson and William streets: U.S. highways 395 and 50. But Dennison only held on to it for a couple of years. It was sold in the summer of 1947 to Roy Brown, who rechristened it the Super Chief V&T Diner the following year. Brown's diner served Coca-Cola alongside "fine food" for breakfast, lunch, and dinner. It specialized in pan fried chicken and even offered tourist information.

A postcard described the Super Chief as "a high class Diner, operated by Mr. & Mrs. Roy Brown on U.S. Highway 395 (on the) North Edge of Carson City, Nevada."

The old railcar stayed in business as a diner until 1958, when it became a pottery shop; later, it served as a moving company office and home to Al's plumbing. It was ultimately donated to the Nevada State Railroad Museum in Carson City.

1947

The Daily Appeal in its former location. *University of Southern California Libraries and California Historical Society*

Journalism

The *Carson Daily Appeal* had been a family operation for something like 80 years. Original editor Henry Mighels started what would later become the state's oldest newspaper in 1865; then he sold it six years later, only to buy it back two years after that.

Mighels's widow published the paper after his death in 1880, and maintained an interest in the company until her death at the age of 100 in 1945. Her son, Henry Mighels Jr., edited the newspaper until 1932.

But in 1947, a new owner took the paper in a new

direction: Arthur Suverkup, owner of the *Gardnerville Record-Courier*, changed the name to the *Carson City Nevada Appeal*, saying the publication covering the state capital should serve "all the people of the state."

Suverkup would sell the newspaper the following year, when it would move from its original building — a stone structure that housed the press and newsroom at Carson and East Second streets — to a new location at 110 West Telegraph Street.

Lodging

A review of rates charged at Carson motels showed visitors to town could expect to pay anywhere from $3 for a single room to four times that rate for a cottage with room for four.

The survey by the *Nevada Appeal* came in response to charges in other newspapers that travelers were being overcharged to stay in the capital.

Rates coming into town from Tonopah or Las Vegas in the south on U.S. 395 were fairly reasonable, with the Capital charging $5 for a single and $6.50 for an apartment. The Aurora had rates of $6 to $8, while the Nevada Auto Court was asking $4, $5, or $6 a night for a room, or $8 for an apartment consisting of a living room, bedroom, and kitchen.

The picture was similar coming in from the north on 395.

The first potential stopping place in town for visitors arriving from Reno, Sparks, or Susanville was the Village Inn, which charged between $8 a night for a couple and a $12 nightly rate for a party of four.

If you decided to look for something better, you'd be rewarded at the next motel on U.S. 395: The DeLux wanted just $3 to $5 for single accommodations and $6 or $6.50 for two. Rates at Taylor Court a little farther on were $6.50 a night for a couple with one child, including "kitchen privileges." A childless couple could spend the night for $5, and a group of four could expect to pay $8.

The Ranch-Otel was a little pricier: $7 for a single, $10 for a double, and $13 for a party of three.

Top: A postcard shows the Carson Motor Lodge in better days. **Above:** It was renamed the Whistle Stop Inn and is seen here shortly before it was demolished. *Author collection, author photo*

The Frontier Motel offered rates of $5 for a single and $10 for a double, while the Carson Motor Lodge, "well inside the city" charged $5 or $6 for a double room, and $10 for a three-bed apartment.

Both the Frontier and the Carson had amenities to recommend them. The Carson (later the Whistle Stop Inn) was shaded by tall trees rising three times as high as its roofline — trees that were, sadly, uprooted in later years. Its rock-walled front office provided a homey feel.

The Frontier, meanwhile, was easy to spot thanks to two huge trees that stood near the entrance and its distinctive neon sign, featuring a cowboy with a neon lasso that flickered to create the illusion that it was spinning. The two large trees were later removed and others planted, and the low stone wall out front was replaced by brick.

The motel had started out as Dorothy's Auto Court, a modest nine-unit establishment with a garage for each visitor and private baths in each room. The auto court, operated by Dorothy and Jonathan Wemyss, was in business by 1939, but five years later, six of its nine cabins were destroyed by fire.

The auto court was closed for the winter, and Dorothy Wemyss was off on a brief vacation in Los Angeles when the fire started around 3 a.m. It wasn't brought under control until two hours later, and although the office wasn't burned, the loss was substantial: Damage was estimated at more than $6,000, including all the furnishings.

Two years later, the Wemysses moved to Santa Barbara and sold the auto court to Floyd Wolverton of Barstow. Sometime shortly after that, it became the Frontier.

An old postcard of the Frontier advertised "family units with kitchenettes if desired," along with a small playground for children and units that were off the street. Proprietors Vance

Lippincott and his wife offered "modern accommodations" complete with "air cooled or heated innerspring mattresses."

Dorothy's Auto Court, top, and its successor, the Frontier Motel. *Author collection*

Pets were accepted, and the motel even offered stalls and a corral for horses, which could be rented for riding. It was still on the outskirts of town.

The Frontier and Mill House Motels in 2022. *Author photos*

By 1959, however, the city was beginning to spread northward. By this time, the Lippincotts had added a two-story wing at the north end, complete with an indoor pool. There were conference and reception rooms, as well, and the motel now had 50 rooms, including bridal suites, family units, and facilities for wheelchairs.

Back in the mid-20th century, motels lined the roadside at the north and south ends of town along U.S. 395 and nearby, but as of this writing, they are fast disappearing. Many, such as the DeLux and Ranch-Otel, have already been torn down and replaced by medical buildings, strip malls, and offices.

Top: The Capitol Motel, which once stood next to the Bank Saloon, is gone today. **Above:** The Hi-Way 50 Motel has been converted into a strip mall. *Top photo by Scott Schrantz; author photo above*

By the spring of 2022, city inspectors had shut down the Frontier, and the former Carson Motor Lodge was chained off, destined to be torn down and replaced by a housing project for unemployed and underemployed residents.

The Mill House, on a frontage road to South Carson Street, was still operating, although the towering sign that once served as a calling card for visitors heading north into the city no longer stands. And the Hi-Way 50 Motel, a block off U.S. 395 on U.S. 50, is still there — but its trees are gone, and it has been transformed into a strip mall.

Politics

R.M. Elston became mayor; he would serve until 1949.

Retail

Wilbur Stodieck opened Wilbur's Men's Shop in the Arlington Hotel. He would move the business to 307 North Carson Street in 1950.

1948

Prison

A new gas chamber was built at Nevada State Prison for executions. Under a law in effect since 1901, the prison was the only place in the state where executions could be conducted, but previous gas executions had been done in a butcher shop at the prison.

In all, 18 executions were performed in the gas chamber through 1979, when the last such death sentence was carried out there.

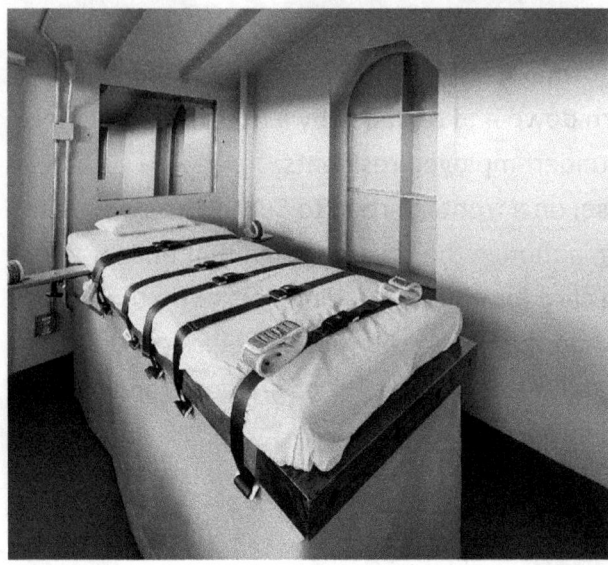

The gas chamber at Nevada State Prison. *Author photo*

1949

Cinema

The south entrance to the State Capitol was used in the comedy *Chicken Every Sunday*, about a married couple played by Celeste Holm and Dan Dailey. Other filming locations included Gardnerville, Minden, Virginia City, and Silver City, as well as the original V&T Railroad.

Health

Carson-Tahoe Hospital opened as a 15-bed medical center on five acres donated by Richard and Ethel Waters.

Politics

Caro Pendegraft became mayor; he would serve until 1951. During his tenure, the city acquired land for Mills Park. Getting the Mills family to donate the land for the city's first park was, he declared, the best thing he did while in office.

"At least I got them 52 acres of park," he said.

Upping the Ante
1950-1959

A postcard shows the Nugget Casino in the 1950s. *Author collection*

1950

Cinema

It was a busy year for moviemakers in and around Carson City, where three new releases were filmed.

The Nevada State Prison was used as the site for *State Penitentiary*, starring Warner Baxter as a businessman falsely accused of embezzlement. And the V&T rail line was featured in a pair of Westerns: *Roar of the Iron Horse* and *Train to Tombstone*.

Fast Food

Dairy Queen opened an outlet at Carson and Sophia streets, just south of the U.S. 395-U.S. 50 intersection.

It would later be rebranded as Dairy Kone when the original eatery moved south to Carson and Fifth. And by the early 1970s, it had another new name: The Penguin, serving a diverse menu that included burgers, hot dogs, and tacos alongside frosties, sundaes, and shakes.

The Penguin, with its blue-circle neon sign, closed in 1997 and was torn down a couple of years after that.

Fire

Winds gusting to 50 miles an hour fanned the flames of a blaze that the *Nevada State Journal* described as the "most dangerous fire on record" in Carson City.

The chef at the Hunter's Lodge discovered the fire around mid-afternoon, when he smelled smoke near the back of the lodge. He went to investigate and saw flames rising 30 feet into the air from a nearby paint and body shop. Upstairs at the lodge, the bar manager was asleep — and dreaming that someone was choking him.

Twenty-four Carson City firefighters responded, using five pieces of equipment to battle the flames. The fire was so intense that three cars at the back of the paint and body shop were melted almost beyond recognition.

Soon, the Hunter's Lodge was engulfed in flames, which spread north along with burning embers carried aloft on the wind. Residents in its path hurried to pour water on their homes, and one resident was badly bruised when he fell from the roof of his house at 112 East Fourth Street.

Sparks ignited a frame building occupied by Lin Yee almost three blocks from the lodge, and it burned to the ground before firefighters could save it. Sagebrush several blocks from the main blaze also caught fire, but it was contained before it could reach any structures.

What was left of the Chinatown district of Carson City, seen here in 1935, was destroyed in the Hunter's Lodge fire. *University of Southern California Libraries and California Historical Society*

The chief of police, Howard Hoffman, had to be treated at Carson-Tahoe Hospital for smoke inhalation.

For the owner of the Hunter's Lodge, it must have felt like deja vu. State Senator Ken Johnson had given leaseholder Hugo Enders an option to buy the building for $50,000 that was scheduled to run out in 12 days. Ten years earlier, Johnson's Senator Café had also been destroyed by fire — just 12 days after he bought it from fellow senator Noble Getchell.

Johnson had recently remodeled the Hunter's Lodge, a historic building that had once been used as a Pony Express stop. He said he only had $15,000 worth of insurance on the Hunter's Lodge, but he said he planned to rebuild it anyway.

Enders suffered significant losses too: He owned all the equipment in the hotel and adjoining lodge, and estimated the damage at $100,000. The paint and body shop, where the fire had started, wound up better off. Damage there was estimated at just $3,000, which was covered by insurance.

Estimates put the total damage at $200,000.

The fire also burned what little remained of Carson City's Chinatown district (bounded by Second and Fourth streets, and Fall and Valley streets) where only six Chinese residents remained. Most of the district was replaced with state buildings such as the Supreme Court, state printing and employment building, and legislative parking garage.

Milestones

Carson City topped 3,000 residents at 3,082 following 24.4 percent growth during the forties.

Politics

Paul Laxalt was elected Ormsby County district attorney. He would serve four years in office.

Switch operator at the Carson train depot in 1940. Arthur Rothstein, Library of Congress

Transportation

The last train on the original Virginia & Truckee Railroad made a final run from Reno to Minden.

Carson Street, showing the Senator Cafe, Western Union Kitzmeyer's Drugs, Standard Station, Victory Club, and other businesses. *UNRS-P1922-01-75, Special Collections and University Archives Department, University of Nevada, Reno*

1951

Business

A new building in downtown Minden housed an insurance company run by partners Warren Reed and Willard Meneley. Two years later, it also served as temporary home to the Douglas County Public Library. Reed's son Alan later opened a restaurant on the site.

Housing

You could rent a four-room furnished house in Carson City for $18 a month, according to a newspaper classified ad.

The Carson Brewery became home to the *Nevada Appeal* in 1951. Author photo

Journalism

A corporation headed by Donald W. Reynolds purchased the *Nevada Appeal* and moved it into a new building... that wasn't new at all.

In fact, the Carson Brewery Co. building at 102 South

Division Street was one of the oldest in town. The two-story structure at the corner of King Street had been built in 1864 to house operations of a four-year-old company that was growing by leaps and bounds.

The company owned by John Wagner brewed "steam beer" (which could be produced without the cold conditions needed to make lager); this was consumed with all due gusto by Comstock miners and shipped as far afield as San Francisco. There was a bar on the bottom floor, and the Masonic Lodge met on the second floor from 1865 up through 1919.

Under new owners Fritz Hagmeyer and Max Stentz, the company had abandoned steam beer in 1913 in favor of a lager they dubbed Tahoe Beer. Soft drink bottling and mineral water from Carson Hot Springs were added to the brewery's menu around the same time.

Tahoe Beer is advertised on the side of a building in Silver City. *Author photo*

But Stentz's son-in-law, Arnold Miller, bought the company in 1926 and liquidated it in 1948, setting the stage for new ownership. That's where the *Nevada Appeal* came in. It had occupied offices on Telegraph Street for just three years when it moved for the second time in its history. In fact, editor Peter Kelley worked in three different buildings between 1945 and 1952.

To go with a new building, the newspaper also purchased a new high-speed roll-fed duplex press. It replaced the sheet press the paper had been using, which required that each page be printed on one side, then turned over and printed on the back.

The newspaper's home in the old brewery proved to be more permanent than its brief stay on Telegraph Street, though: It would continue to operate at that location until late 1974.

Politics

Wilbur Stodieck, owner of Wilbur's Men's Shop, became mayor.

1952

Retail

Around the first of May, the Stone Market at 513 North Carson Street was offering two pounds of bananas for 33 cents, picnic hams for 39 cents, colored hens for 53 cents, a dozen fresh ranch eggs for 55 cents, Wesson oil for 57 cents, and oven-ready turkeys for 65 cents.

"We hate high prices too," a newspaper ad declared.

1953

Cinema

The Sky-Vue Drive-In opened May 1 along U.S. 395 at the north end of Carson City with a single screen and spaces for 300 cars.

Two years later, owners George Gessler and Cecil Perrin

placed a historic Virginia & Truckee train on display along the highway next to the theater.

The owners also publicized the theater with promotions such as a "Chevrolet Night," in which anyone in a Chevy was admitted free for a showing of the Western *Destry*, starring Audie Murphy and Marie Blanchard. The promotion was sponsored (naturally) by the local Chevy dealer, C.C. Chevrolet.

Gessler sold the theater to Carson Theatre owner Charles Leonard in 1959, with Gessler moving on to another venture: a casino.

The Sky-Vue continued operating until around 1963, when plans were announced to build a shopping center on the site, to be anchored by Sewell's Market.

1954

The second Carson Theatre is seen in 1954, the year it opened.
dallasmovietheaters, cinematreasures, Creative Commons.

Cinema

The second Carson Theatre opened at West Washington and North Carson streets.

More than 600 patrons could fill the theater to watch CinemaScope movies on its 42-foot-wide screen. Most of the seating (584) was on the main orchestra floor, with 64 more seats available in the loge section and 15 in a "cry room" next to the projection box.

After the theater closed, it was transformed into the Silver Spike Casino and, after that, was remodeled to become the Washington Street Station office building.

Dining

Forty state highway department employees gathered to honor office managers from Ely, Reno, and Las Vegas in a luncheon at Enrico's, a popular place for business and club meetings.

Organizations like the Women's Republican Club of Reno met there for lunch during a visit to the state legislature. But it wasn't a partisan business: Later that same year, Democratic Women's Club representatives gathered there to plan organizing into a state unit.

The restaurant even sponsored its own golf tournament in the early sixties.

Former Reno waiter Henry Ramirez had started the business as Dolly's Snack Bar, named for his wife, but by the mid-1950s had transformed it into Enrico's.

For many years the only Carson City restaurant specializing in Italian food, Enrico's also offered buffet-style chuck wagon dinners for $2 in 1956. Lunches were reasonably priced but featured generous portions and were served on white table linens.

The "dinners deluxe" menu included items ranging from veal scaloppini to spaghetti and meatballs, from New York Steak to Lamb Chops. A selection of wines took up much of the menu space.

Located next to the Carson Theater, it was open from 5 to 9 p.m. weekdays (except Wednesdays, when it was closed) and from 3 to 9 on Sundays.

The building later became a podiatrist's office.

Fire Station No. 1 opened on Musser one block west of Carson Street in 1954. *Photo by Scott Schrantz*

Fire

A new fire station opened at 111 North Curry Street at Musser, after the Warren Engine Company outgrew the station across the street. It remained in use for four decades, first by the all-volunteer Warren Engine Company and then by the Carson Fire Department until it moved to a five-bay station on Stewart Street.

The Curry Street station was ultimately demolished in 2005.

The building it replaced, ironically, still stands. Built in 1864, it has undergone extensive remodeling and is now part of the Secretary of State's office.

The first Warren Fire Station, replaced in 1954, is seen at left in 1940 and above today, after its conversion into offices. *Top: Author photo; left: Arthur Rothstein, Library of Congress*

The Nugget Casino at night. *Author photo*

Gaming

Richard Graves leased Brockerick's Bar and the Mint Café in February and combined the operations, opening the Carson City Nugget on March 1. It was an immediate success — so much so that he would pay $200,000 to build another Nugget, which opened just a year later with 50 slot machines and a 60-stool café at Twelfth and B streets in Sparks.

It eventually expanded into a pair of high-rise towers.

Like Peter Piersante, who later bought the Senator Club and renamed it Cactus Jack's, Graves had come from Idaho, where he'd been involved in the dining and gaming businesses. In his case, he'd been selling and operating pinball and slot machines, in addition to owning restaurants in Boise, Caldwell, Coeur D'Alene, Kimberly, Mountain Home, and Sandpoint. Graves even had Boise artist Roscoe "Duke" Reading design a mascot for his Last Chance Café in the Boise suburb of Garden City. The mascot, a prospector holding a nugget and a pan of gold, was named, fittingly, Last Chance Joe.

But Graves's Idaho endeavors came to a screeching halt when that state outlawed gambling in 1953.

So he sold all his businesses there, pulled up stakes and brought Last Chance Joe with him in a move to Nevada, where he bought the Eagle Club and Café in Yerington and rechristened it the Nugget.

He brought something else with him, too: the recipe for a burger he'd served as his Coeur d'Alene restaurant, the Brunswick Café. Known as the Awful Awful Burger because it was "awful big and awful good" (though possibly not awful good for you). The two-patty tower comes served with onion, tomato, and lettuce on an onion bun in a basket with a pound of fries. It was first served for 60 cents at the Little Nugget on Virginia Street in Reno, which Graves opened with partner Jim Kelly in 1953, taking over an establishment formerly known as the Piccadilly.

Carson City was next on Graves's radar screen.

There was some question about whether Carson City was big enough to support a casino, and the Nugget on Carson

Street was initially a small-scale operation. But within a few months, Graves was planning a second addition to the casino; he sold the Reno operation to Kelly but kept on grilling his Awful Awful Burgers at the Carson Nugget, which as of this writing is one of two places you can still get it. (The other is Jim Kelly's Nugget in Crystal Bay at Lake Tahoe.)

The Awful Awful Burger, served at the Carson Nugget. *Author photo*

Despite Graves's misgivings about the size of Carson City, "the Carson Nugget took right off," he said in a 1978 interview with the University of Nevada's Oral History Program. "It was very surprising to me because Carson was a sleepy town. There wasn't much business in town."

The Nugget, however, didn't just cater to locals. Its location on U.S. 395 at the heart of town made it a natural drawing card.

In Carson, Graves commissioned a 4-foot-high wooden

replica of Last Chance Joe, who'd become a fixture in ads for every Nugget casino Graves opened. The wooden figure was used at a number of publicity events and became so popular, Graves used the character as the basis for a line of dolls eventually made by the Rempel toy company and sold for $1.98 at the Nugget gift shop.

Left: A giant version of Last Chance Joe stands tall in Sparks. **Below:** A drawing on a 60th anniversary box in the author's collection. *Author photos*

A much bigger version of Last Chance Joe, standing 36 feet tall, was placed at the entrance to the Sparks Nugget opposite a giant chicken advertising Kentucky Fried Chicken in the casino's Golden Rooster restaurant.

Graves held on to the Carson Nugget for three years, then sold it to Hop and Howard Adams. The brothers not only expanded the operation by purchasing adjacent buildings along Carson Street north to Robinson Street, but they also added the distinctive corner sign, patterned after one used at the Las Vegas Golden Nugget.

An interesting side note: Graves's attorney was none other than Paul Laxalt, future founder of the Ormsby House casino and a close friend of Ronald Reagan who served as governor of Nevada from 1967 to 1971 and U.S. senator from 1974 to 1987.

1955

Flooding

The Carson River went on a rampage, demolishing bridges and flooding farmland through the Carson Valley region. At least 1,000 people were left temporarily homeless in western Nevada, with initial damage estimates topping $5 million.

Power and phone service to Gardnerville and Minden were out for prolonged periods. And while road crews managed to keep Highway 395 open between Reno and Carson City, the road was still submerged in several places.

In the aftermath of the flooding, Governor Charles Russell asked President Eisenhower to declare a 10,000-square-mile swath of western Nevada a major disaster area.

Gaming

The Silver Spur Casino, offering slot machines and table games, opened in an old 19th century brick building a couple of blocks south of the Senator Bar at Carson and Proctor streets.

An early postcard labeled it "The Friendly House of

Action" and "Your Best Bet," serving "the finest food in Nevada" and offering a saloon and Keno betting.

A vintage postcard for the Silver Spur Casino. *Author collection*

Politics

Turner Houston, a 31-year-old manager of the Sprouse-Reitz store, was elected mayor of Carson City with 456 votes, 56 more than runner-up Robert Tolson.

Houston would serve as mayor for the next six years.

Prostitution

Chuck LeMond, a former pimp from Sacramento, opened the Moonlight Ranch brothel on the western edge of Lyon County in Mound House, just east of Carson City.

Joe Conforte, who would later own the Starlight Ranch in Mound House and the famous Mustang Ranch in Washoe County, arrived in Nevada this same year.

1956

Education

A new $400,000 high school opened on land donated by rancher John Winters at 1140 West King Street. Within two decades, it would be replaced by a newer campus at Saliman Road and U.S. Highway 50, with the old school taking on a new identity as Carson Junior High.

1959

Gaming

The First National Bank building at Carson and Telegraph streets was sold to attorney William Crowell, who promptly leased the first floor of the building to George Gessler Jr. and his wife to be used as the Kit Carson Casino.

Gessler had previously operated Hunter's Lodge.

Plans called for the casino at 402 North Carson Street to include a bar and hofbräu restaurant and to feature an early Western motif. Gessler was redecorating the place in an antique cedar finish, and a life-size statue of Kit Carson was placed at the building's entrance.

The 24-hour casino would feature entertainment and dancing nightly, with meals served from 11 a.m. to 2 a.m. in the hofbräu and breakfast served after that.

The bank, meanwhile, was moving into a new building two blocks to the north.

The Kit Carson Casino would operate until the late sixties, with the Horseshoe Club later taking over the spot.

The Carson Valley Drug Store building in Minden. *Author photo*

Retail

The Carson Valley Drug Store opened in a new building erected in downtown Minden. Bill Rahnke operated the pharmacy inside the mercantile at that location; it was sold in 1963 to Jim and Jane Stratton, who continued at that location until they moved to Gardnerville in 1977.

Sports

Carson City didn't have its own baseball team, but the town got its own special "Carson City Night" up in Reno on August 29, when the Silver Sox hosted Fresno in a minor-league game.

You could get tickets to the game at the chamber of commerce, Cathey's Shoe Tree, Ken's Flying A Service, the Globe Saloon, Dutch Mill, Kitzmeyer's Drugs, Meyers Hardware, Tim's Liquor, Western Auto, Union Federal, and Murdock's Clothing.

CARSON CITY CENTURY

Growing Capital
1960-1969

A postcard shows businesses along Carson Street including Sprouse-Reitz, Kitzmeyer's Drugs, and the Silver Spur Casino. *Author collection*

1960

Law

Carson City lawyer Paul Laxalt represented Nugget Casino owner Richard Graves in a unique case that gave him something to crow about.

Graves had installed a 14-pound gold statue of a rooster in his Sparks casino. The rooster was "arrested" and taken into custody because of his gold plumage: It was against the law at the time, under the Gold Reserve Act, for most Americans to possess gold unless it was in their jewelry, teeth, or some kinds of art.

The feds put the rooster "behind bars" in a California bank vault, and it actually faced trial in *United States v. One Solid Gold Object In Form of A Rooster*. Laxalt, however, won the case for Graves, who was allowed to spring the rooster from his vault and return it to the lobby of his Sparks casino.

The jury needed a day and a half of deliberations before setting the jailbird free. It remained at the casino until 2013, when it was sold in an auction for $234,000.

The other half of the postcard shown on the previous page shows the Senator Café on Carson Street.

Author collection

Milestones

Carson City's growth was accelerating with the baby boom. The city was two-thirds larger than it had been just a decade earlier, hitting a new high of 5,163 residents.

1961

Basketball

Carson High fell to Rancho in the AA state finals 60-51.

Bowling

Silver State Lanes opened in Carson City.

Politics

Motel owner A.A. Autrand became Carson City's mayor, winning a five-way race easily with 446 votes.

1963

Crime

Frank Sinatra's son had been kidnapped, but he turned up safe and sound at a Carson City service station.

Just days after the assassination of John F. Kennedy, 19-year-old Frank Sinatra Jr. had been abducted at gunpoint from Harrah's Club Lodge in Lake Tahoe by one Barry Keenan, who was demanding $240,000 in ransom.

Keenan wasn't a total stranger. The UCLA student, 23, had known Nancy Sinatra (Frank Sinatra Jr.'s sister) in grade school. Lately, he'd fallen on hard times: A back injury had left him in severe pain, and he'd become addicted to painkillers that left him bankrupt.

His solution?

Kidnap Frank Jr.

"I decided upon Junior because Frank Sr. was tough, and I had friends whose parents were in show business, and I knew Frank always got his way," Keenan told *New Times Los Angeles*. "It wouldn't be morally wrong to put him through a few hours of grief worrying about his son."

Keenan and an accomplice, high school friend Joe Amsler, confronted Frank Jr. at the singer's hotel, where he was eating chicken with a member of his band, trumpet player John Foss. They tied Foss up, but he got loose and immediately called police.

Keenan, meanwhile, issued his demand for $240,000.

Calls were placed to the Carson City service station across from the Capitol, where the elder Sinatra was evidently told to receive them. Four calls came in before he arrived, however, each taken by Dan McStay, who thought he was being pranked — until Sinatra Sr. showed up with another man, whom McStay believed to be an FBI agent.

"That's when I figured the guy I had been talking to was probably one of the kidnappers," McStay later said. "I was quite concerned. I was afraid by being as abrupt as I had been, perhaps he wouldn't call back anymore."

McStay said Sinatra "obviously didn't want to be recognized. He had on a dark coat, with the collar turned up."

When the next call came, Sinatra took it and started writing on a piece of paper his companion had given him. Sinatra ultimately paid the $240,000 ransom, which the FBI left at a location specified by another accomplice, John Irwin.

Keenan retrieved it and appeared to have gotten away with his scheme. But Irwin, who was hightailing it out of there to disappear in New Orleans, stopped to visit his brother in San

Diego. The loose-lipped Irwin told his brother what they'd done, and the brother tipped authorities. All three men were in custody by the end of the day.

Keenan ended up serving 4½ years in prison, while the two others each served 3½.

Milestones

Carson City's population growth robbed it of a title it had worn for years: that of the nation's smallest state capital. Montpelier, Vermont, was now smaller. By 2020, Carson had grown so large it wasn't even in the bottom 10 anymore, ranking 37th overall, ahead of Charleston, West Virginia, and just behind Cheyenne, Wyoming.

Politics

James Robertson, a furniture store operator, defeated incumbent A.A. Autrand for mayor decisively, 1,133 votes to 470. Robertson would serve as mayor until 1969.

1964

Auto Racing

The Tahoe-Carson Speedway, or T-Car, as it was often known, opened in August on a 17-acre piece of land just south of the Stewart Indian School.

The one-third-mile track included bleacher seating for 3,000 spectators, who were shielded from the action by a 12-foot chain-link fence. It was all the work of Bob Meyer, who owned the land, and his partner in the track, Jim Owen.

The first event, a benefit for injured driver Arlan Robinson, was planned for August 23 under the auspices of the Reno

Stock Car Association. The RSCA planned to run claimers, modifieds, and super modifieds every Sunday, with the sprint car racing in the future, Meyer said.

Sadly, Robinson died later that month. The Reno driver's car had hit another car flipped during a race in Plumas County, California. He survived nearly two weeks before his death.

The speedway, which was also called Silver State Raceway and Champion Motor Speedway over the years, operated until 2005, when it was closed to make way for a housing development that fell through. (There is housing out there now, although the main street in the area retains the name Race Track Road.)

Standout racers over the years included Fred Allen, a Fallon-area driver who won track championships in 1977 and again in 1980, and Dave Lester, who won four track championships between 1977 and 2001.

Lester once finished ahead of Derrike Cope at T-Car; Cope would win the Daytona 500 in 1990.

Dining

The Pine Cone Restaurant announced it had reopened in Carson City, serving the "finest Chinese and American dishes," including "special family dinners" at 301 North Carson Street, on the corner of Proctor.

The restaurant was open from 6 a.m. to 10 p.m., and takeout was available.

The Pine Cone had been a popular hangout for high school kids in the 1950s. Later on, Nevada Supreme Court Justice John Collins would stop in almost nightly for dinner. Governor Mike O'Callaghan, who walked there from the governor's mansion, was a regular for breakfast.

The Pine Cone's motto was "Just Good Food."

The Fireside Inn and 19-room Greeno Hotel, owned by Hal and Margie Greeno, was just behind the Pine Cone on Proctor Street. An early postcard described the Greeno as "Carson City's Newest and Most Modern… Famous for its adjoining 'Fireside Inn.' Where Western Hospitality is Genuine."

Part of the two-story building with a large basement was built around 1948, and the Greeno was open by the following year. It advertised itself as a place where divorcees were welcome, and hot tubs were added to the rooms in the 1980s.

The business was also rumored to have hosted events such as women's mud wrestling. And on one occasion, a patron who had won a 20-pound pig in a fireman's ball raffle set it free in the building, Mayor Marv Teixeira recalled. The place was full at the time, so the pig caused quite a commotion, but the animal was eventually retrieved.

Despite such colorful incidents the Fireside Inn restaurant had a reputation for serving good food, and state legislators would frequent the bar for drinks.

Frank and Nadine Prior bought the business in 1962.

The building's distinctive green roof wasn't universally popular: In the late 1990s, Mayor Ray Masayko said it clashed with the building's brick walls. (The barstool cushions in the Fireside Inn were green, too).

Masayko's comments came years after the establishment closed its doors for good in 1986, when the bank took over from then-owner Jack Lawry, who'd been hit with financial problems and couldn't keep it open.

Politics

Carson City lawyer Paul Laxalt's first run for U.S. Senate ended in defeat, but not by much. TV networks called the race in Laxalt's favor on election night, but late-reporting districts ultimately delivered victory to incumbent Howard Cannon by a paltry 48-vote margin.

Transportation

U.S. Highway 395 north of Carson City became the first section of the road to be converted into a freeway.

1965

Cinema

Leonard Nimoy wasn't quite ready to explore the galaxy on *Star Trek* when he headed the cast of *Deathwatch*, an independent film directed by Vic Morrow and set in the 1930s. The Nevada State Prison doubled as the film's French prison.

It was one of the first movies to be marketed specifically to gay audiences and never shown widely in theaters.

Lodging

The 1960s brought a new trend combining the convenience of a motel with the central location of a hotel. Out of this trend was born the City Center Motel, a new four-story lodge in the heart of the city at 800 North Carson Street.

"Unique or utilitarian?" an ad in the *Nevada State Journal* asked. "Carson City's new City Center Motel is both."

Owner and developer C.E. Babbitt's big hook to potential guests was electricity. Two years earlier, he'd built the first all-electric apartment building in Boise, Idaho, and he was using that template on the Carson project.

Climate control was a big part of his pitch too. Guests could heat or cool their own rooms individually, and a master control near the office allowed the manager to adjust the settings when rooms weren't in use.

The City Center Motel is known as the Carson Tahoe Hotel today. *Author photo*

"We eliminated costly piping and ductwork," Babbitt explained. "We turned more floor space into useable room space because we didn't have to install a boiler. Without a boiler, there is no 'major maintenance,' only individual room maintenance which doesn't disrupt the entire motel operation."

Double-paned windows and extra insulation shielded guests in the motel's 89 rooms from the cold winter nights. The motel also featured a heated pool and sundeck. It all represented what Babbitt called "a sizeable investment in 'people comfort,' but our business is people, Very Important People, and we wanted them to have the finest."

The motel held a grand opening celebration in June.

Politics

Lieutenant Governor Paul Laxalt was elected governor by 6,000 votes, defeating two-term incumbent Grant Sawyer.

Paul Laxalt stands in front of Governor's Mansion in 1967. *UNRS-P2015-12-00054, Special Collections and University Archives Department, University of Nevada, Reno*

Retail

Carson City may still have been small as cities go, but it wasn't far from the cutting edge of that hot new trend in retail: the indoor mall. Many larger cities didn't have one yet, but the new $3 million Carson Mall held its formal opening in March at Carson and Stewart streets.

The new center was anchored at its south end by a Gray Reid's store with 52 departments spread across 60,000 square feet. That was more than one-third of the mall's 165,000 square feet of space, making it the shopping center's largest tenant. The Reno-based department store had been founded by Joseph H. Gray and Hosea E. Reid in the early 1900s, and the company would stay in business until 1986.

Carson Mall had 35 tenants in all, with a new Safeway outlet taking up 25,000 square feet at the north end of the property. Gray Reid's and Safeway were connected by a 380-foot enclosed, landscaped corridor that was home to 30 other businesses and offices. Two service stations and a Dayton Tire and Auto Service Center also set up shop at the mall.

Carson Mall, seen from the air in 1973. *UNRS-P1992-01-1152, Special Collections and University Archives Department, University of Nevada, Reno*

Other notable stores included a Sprouse-Reitz five-and-dime store, Mode O'Day dress shop, and Swenson's ice cream parlor. There was a fabric shop, paint shop, gift shop, a couple of shoe stores (and a shoe repair shop), paint shop, barber, beauty salon, real estate office, camera shop, dry cleaners, laundry, banks, and a jeweler.

If you were hungry, you could visit the Chicken Box or the George C. Huff restaurant (which also had a billiard parlor). ...

Jack's Bar, aka the Bank Saloon, at Fifth and Carson. *Author photo*

Jack's Bar opened at Fifth and Carson streets, but it wasn't the first bar to occupy the building. In fact, the sandstone structure on the corner dates all the way back to 1899, when it opened as the Bank Saloon.

It went through a series of owners and name changes during the first half of the 20th century, doing business as the Bank Resort, Hernando's Hideaway, the Y-NOT Bar, and Angelo's before morphing into Jack's Bar.

1966

Basketball

The Stewart Indian School won its first state championship on the court, claiming the A Division title with a 62-59 victory over Moapa Valley. Danny Lee led the Braves with 24 points in their first championship game appearance since 1939.

The Carson Valley Appeal labeled the game "the big freeze," noting that the Stewart team "rolled the ball, stood in place for 30 seconds at a time" and scored many of its points at the free-throw line.

Stewart, which dropped just one game all season, had advanced to the finals with a 71-60 win over Virgin Valley. Lee led the way with 20 points as Stewart bolted out to an 18-15 lead and outscored its opponents in each of the four quarters.

Over the course of two seasons, the Braves won 23 games in a row before the streak ended in their final game of 1966 with a 77-69 loss to Virginia City High School.

Stewart had a secret weapon: They could communicate without the other teams knowing what they were saying, by using native languages.

"Nobody understood us," said Rupert Steele, who attended Stewart a few years later. "Just like the code talkers, you know?"

Lodging

The historic Arlington Hotel on the 500 block of North Carson Street met its end. The hotel, which took up most of the block between Robinson and Spear streets, had become run down, and renovations were deemed too costly, so the owners demolished the entire block.

It's now the site of the Carson Nugget's western parking lot.

1968

Business

First National Bank of Nevada, which had purchased Farmer's Bank in 1954, moved into a new building in Minden. It later was remodeled to house an engineering firm.

The then-new Carson-Tahoe Hospital replaced the old facility, which was destroyed by fire as the new one was being built. *Author photo*

Fire

Construction well was under way on a new Carson-Tahoe Hospital when the old hospital just 30 yards away burned down August 26.

In a way, the new hospital may have been responsible for the demise of the old one: A contractor was burning construction debris at the new site when the wind began to gust, carrying embers onto the shake roof of the existing facility.

About 50 firefighters were dispatched to battle the blaze in the building, which had been built as a private hospital in 1949 and become a public facility in 1964. The fire started shortly after noon, just after the completion of one surgery, and another operation was about to begin, but all 32 patients in the 34-bed facility were evacuated safely. The woman about to have surgery was already anesthetized and, when she woke up, found herself in Reno.

Billows of flame shot upward through the wooden roof of

the brick-walled building, fueled by oxygen that ran through copper piping in the attic that came apart during the fire. The only injuries were to three firefighters who suffered smoke inhalation.

The old building was a complete loss, with the value of the structure and its contents pegged at $400,000, most of it due to water damage.

Many patients were moved temporarily into houses across the street, and the obstetrics department was transferred to the Stewart Indian School until the new hospital could be completed. Fortunately, that didn't take long: The new facility opened in November, just three months after the fire.

Gaming

The city had a new ambassador.

In neon.

"The Senator," a two-story-tall figure perched halfway up the roofline on the old Senator Bar, welcomed visitors to town at the southwest corner of Carson and Spear streets.

Decked out in a black coat, red vest, and tan pants with a matching black-and-red hat, The Senator wears his white hair long to match his flowing mustache, but at night he lights up all in red — even the green bills in his outstretched hand marked with the word "Howdy."

In earlier days, The Senator was dressed all in a cream-colored outfit with the exception of a gold vest and hat trim. His arm was animated, moving up and down.

The Senator was installed as part of the business' expansion, coinciding with a name change to Mike's Senator Club.

1969

Government

Carson City got a whole lot bigger, geographically speaking, when the state legislature approved a measure to consolidate the city and Ormsby County. Under the measure, Carson City became Nevada's only jurisdiction to consist of a combined city and county government.

Ormsby County ceased to exist on July 1, and the city limits of Carson City were expanded to cover its former territory. The "new" Carson City covered nearly 147 square miles and included Snow Peak, rising 9,274 feet in the Sierra Nevada. Still, it's a far cry from the size of the largest U.S. city, Sitka, Alaska, which sprawls out over 2,870 square miles.

The consolidation saved money ($7,200, to be exact) by reducing the number of elected officials from eight to five. It was, in actuality, just the final step in a process that had been ongoing since 1951, when some city and county departments had been consolidated. A little more than a decade later, all departments had been combined.

After the merger was complete under the new measure, just one distinction remained:

"People in Carson City wanted a leash law," City Manager Henry Etchemendy said. "People in the rural area didn't."

Politics

Eugene Scrivner, a chiropractor, was elected mayor of Carson City.

Retail

The Carson Mall's Gray Reid's store — which had opened with so much fanfare as the main anchor just three years earlier — was closed.

The store's owner, Stuart Webb, admitted that demand in the Carson City market simply wasn't enough to sustain a store the size of Gray Reid's. But that didn't stop another company with a store in Reno from jumping in to fill the void. The company was known as Disco (short for "discount" — there were no mirror balls or Bee Gees records; that craze still lay in the future). It had nearly a dozen other stores across the country when it moved into the old Gray Reid's space.

Entrance to the Carson Mall in 2022. *Author photo*

The new store was stocked with $1 million worth of merchandise in about 20 departments, and had a double row of slot machines.

Customers from five counties converged on the new Disco for its opening day in early December. One of them apparently got lost amid the throngs, and his wife had to petition the store for help in locating him: "Robert Brown, you are lost and your wife is waiting for you at the wig counter," came the loudspeaker announcement.

(Perhaps he'd checked there already when she was trying on a wig and hadn't recognized her.)

CARSON CITY CENTURY

The Wages of Sin
1970-1979

The Ormsby House hotel and casino raised Carson City's skyline in 1972. *Author photo*

1970

Milestones

Carson City's population soared by nearly 200 percent in the 1960s to 15,468.

1971

Education

Western Nevada Community College opened its doors to students in Carson City on September 19, two years after the

Nevada State Legislature created the community college system. (Colleges were also established in Clark County and Northern Nevada at Elko.)

The state made preliminary plans to accept 190 full-time-equivalent students.

The Carson City Board of Supervisors voted to lease the old Civic Auditorium to the state for two classrooms and three administrative offices. As part of a $50,000 grant, the city made $8,000 in internal improvements to the building so classrooms could be created on the first floor and spent $10,000 to equip a secretarial science classroom.

Meanwhile, the state adopted a policy under which any student graduating from a community college would be admitted to the University of Nevada as a regular student and given transfer credit for community college coursework.

Gaming

Milos "Sharkey" Begovich purchased the Golden Bubble Casino in Gardnerville. The property had been the site of a corner saloon built in the late 1890s. (Surrounding businesses back then included a blacksmith shop, mortuary, and drugstore.)

Begovich earned his nickname when his mom ran a boarding house in Plymouth, California, during his youth. "The house was full of Slavic foreigners," he told the *Reno Gazette-Journal*. "So when Jack Sharkey, who was Slavic, became the boxing champion of the world, the men just started calling me Sharkey."

The *Gazette-Journal* described Begovich as a "fight fan, clown fan, Indian fan, gambler, restaurateur and casino owner."

He'd started out running a gambling operation in Jackson,

California in the late 1940s. Gaming wasn't closely watched, so the town had nine casinos: "There was more gambling at the time than in Carson City." No slot machines, but table games like 21, roulette, and craps.

Eventually, the police cracked down on his operation, so he moved to Lake Tahoe, becoming a dealer and later a pit boss at Harrah's before striking out on his own. He tried to start a club overseas in Seoul, South Korea, but that didn't work out, so he returned to Nevada.

Sharkey's Casino in Gardnerville started out as Sharkey's Nugget, but it was the Golden Bubble before that. *Author photo*

After spending some more time in Tahoe, where he was part-owner of the Tahoe Nugget, he learned the Gardnerville casino was available and purchased it, initially calling it Sharkey's Nugget before shortening the name to Sharkey's.

Begovich had the market to himself: The nearest casino was 14 miles away. Sharkey's wasn't huge, with three blackjack tables and some slot machines in the late 1970s, but he turned the casino into more than a gambling house, creating an unofficial museum stocked with artifacts from the Old West.

He also displayed pictures of prizefighters and boxing memorabilia, like the gloves from an epic lightweight title fight between Joe Gans and Battling Nelson from 1906 down the road in Goldfield.

He even staged the first fight in Gardnerville. His Cow Pasture Festival boxing shows were mainstays in the community for years. Up to 2,000 fans would crowd into metal folding chairs and, as of 1988, anted up $8 to $16 to watch the pros duke it out in a ring set up on the town ballfield. (The cow pasture was on the other side of the fence).

Sharkey's was famous for its inch-thick prime rib, which was served alongside free-flowing beer at the festival and at the casino itself. In '71, you could get a dinner built around inch-thick prime rib for $3.95. Or you could wait until the holidays, when Begovich served up a free Serbian Christmas feast. One year, in 1977, he cooked 25 suckling pigs and 25 goats to feed 3,000 people.

Over the years, country music stars such as Willie Nelson and Waylon Jennings would appear onstage at Sharkey's.

Running a small casino, Begovich told the *Gazette-Journal*, is "1,000 times more challenging than running a big casino. The guy in a big one works his shift and goes home. Not me. I'm always here."

Sharkey would own the casino for three decades, finally selling it in 2001, shortly before his death. ...

The Senator Club became Cactus Jack's Senator Club when it was sold to Peter Piersanti. Cactus Pete, as he was known, had started out in the early 1950s owning Island Park Lodge, not far from Yellowstone National Park.

The lodge had featured a number of slot machines, but

when the state outlawed gambling in 1953, Piersanti pulled up stakes and relocated just south of the Nevada state line, where he opened Cactus Pete's Casino and founded the community of Jackpot.

The Senator Club became Cactus Jack's in 1971.
Author photo

When he bought the Senator Club, he moved to Carson City and operated it until he retired 18 years later. He died in February 1994 at the age of 77. ...

The State Legislative Building was completed in 1971. Author photo

Government

Work was completed on a new 96,000-square-foot State Legislative Building.

Prostitution

Mustang Ranch owner Joe Conforte persuaded Washoe County officials to pass an ordinance that would allow the licensing of brothels — effectively shielding them from raids and closures.

Las Vegas officials, fearing that Conforte might make a similar play in Clark County, hurried to the legislature with a proposal that prostitution be banned by state law in counties with more than a specified number of residents. At the time, only Clark County qualified.

But the ban had the effect of opening up the rest of Nevada to the world's oldest profession. All brothel owners had to do was persuade local officials to allow it, which is, not surprisingly, exactly what they did. (A state law enacted in 1979 specified that brothels could not be advertised in counties where they were prohibited.)

Ten Nevada counties allowed brothels to operate as of 2018, most of them in rural areas. They're not legal in Carson City, or in Washoe County, home to Reno. But anyone in Carson looking for the kind of services a brothel provides doesn't have far to go: Four of the state's 20 legal brothels are just over the hill in the Lyon County community of Mound House to the east.

The Old Globe Saloon got a new home on Curry Street after being in business since 1951. Originally founded in 1875, it was closed for Prohibition in 1918 and later revived. *Author photo*

Refreshments

The Old Globe Saloon moved to Curry Street from Carson Street, with the new structure designed by Nevada state bridge engineer Hector Puccinelli to replicate the original establishment. The original stone ice house, built in 1890, was also incorporated in the building.

The Globe had been in business since all the way back in 1875, when it had been opened by French Canadian brothers Andrew and Henry Robert. Shut down for Prohibition in 1918, it had been given a second life in 1951 when Andrew Robert's grandson, Bob Golightly, asked Virgil Bucchianeri Sr. to reopen it.

Bucchianeri ran the Globe until 1994, when his grandson Hector took over and spent several thousand dollars over the next couple of years on a facelift and renovations. The upgrades helped the bar's image, he told the *Reno Gazette-Journal*: "We had kind of a rough crowd when I got here. We thinned some of that out."

Television

Barbara Eden and Larry Hagman weren't playing Jeannie and Major Nelson when they teamed up for *A Howling in the Woods*. The made-for-TV mystery was filmed in Carson City, Dayton, Genoa, and Glenbrook.

1972

Gaming

Paul Laxalt finished out a single term as governor in 1971 and stayed in Carson City, where he opened the Ormsby House a year later. It wasn't the original Ormsby House, a hotel and saloon built by Major William Ormsby in 1860 that became known as the Park Hotel in the early 1900s.

That hotel, touted as "headquarters for tourists and commercial travelers," faced competition from the newer St. Charles Hotel and, at some point, became a flophouse before going dark in 1919. That's where the Laxalt family came in, purchasing the property in 1932 and having it torn down not long afterward.

But that wasn't the end of the Ormsby House name or the Laxalt family's involvement.

In 1972, the former governor applied the storied name to a new hotel and casino in the heart of Carson City: the tallest building in town at 600 South Carson Street. Boasting 220 hotel rooms, the hotel was sold to Hawthorne gaming operator Woody Loftin in 1976, and Loftin's son Truett took over upon his death in the mid-eighties.

The Ormsby House did decent business until the advent of tribal casinos in California started draining business, and it closed in 1993 amid bankruptcy proceedings.

The original Ormsby House, seen here decked out for the Fourth of July at the turn of the century.

Prostitution

Lyon County officially licensed four brothels under a new county ordinance that legalized houses of prostitution: the Moonlight, Sagebrush, Starlight, and Kit Kat ranches.

The late 1950s and '60s had seen a series of raids on houses of prostitution, which survived each attempt to shut them down because of their popularity and the willingness of law enforcement to look the other way — if the price was right. But now, under the new ordinance, the brothels and the county government had reached a sort of détente.

A billboard points the way to Mound House brothels, adult entertainment, and other businesses off U.S. 50 east of Carson City. *Author photo*

The ordinance, approved in March, called for brothels with six or fewer workers to pay a $1,000 monthly fee, and required prostitutes to get weekly medical checkups.

Lyon County limited the number of brothel licenses it issued to four, all of them in Mound House just west of the Carson City limits.

Sheriff George Allen said each of the four approved

houses of prostitution had undergone extensive background checks before being approved. But if Joe Conforte, owner of the Starlight, is to be believed, Allen had ample reason to back the brothels.

In his book *Breaks, Brains, and Balls*, Conforte wrote: "Every month I used to give Kitty and Julius Bunkowski money to pay off the sheriff, George Allen, and whoever else was on the take at that time in Lyon County." (Kitty Bono, who later owned Kitty's Guest House, was a 50-50 partner with Conforte at the Starlight Ranch.) "But when it got legalized, I said, 'What the hell do I need to pay you guys for? Now it's legal.' So I stopped paying them."

Weather

Carson City recorded its highest temperature in city history, 103 degrees, on August 8. That same year, on December 11, it got the coldest it's ever gotten, dropping to 18 below zero.

1973

Gaming

The closed Kit Carson Casino reopened as the Horseshoe Club, founded by Eugene Chaney Jr.

He would run the club until his death in 2007.

The casino actually took in three buildings along North Carson Street, running north from the corner of Telegraph Street to 412 North Carson, just south of Cactus Jack's. The casino spanned the ground floor of all three buildings; the second floor was taken up by 10 offices and five apartments.

In the mid-20th century, the center building on Carson Street had housed a Rexall pharmacy called Miller's Drugs alongside a place called Corbett & Hancock's Ship Bar, which was notable because its doorway was shaped like the bow of a ship jutting out onto the sidewalk. A postcard for the bar boasted that it had on display "the wheel and lights of the old Mary Hatch, which was sunk in Monterey Bay 120 years ago."

The Ship Bar was long gone by the time the Horseshoe Club came along.

The Horseshoe Club Casino in 2013, two years before it closed. *Photo by Scott Schrantz*

A 1981 ad for the casino touted a snack bar, bingo, blackjack, and slots that "pay up to 97 percent." Billed as the "home of the 50-cent drink" (what kind of drink wasn't mentioned), its slogan was "Friendliest Atmosphere in the West."

In 1995, they were still serving an 89-cent breakfast there.

The casino closed for good in 2015 and was remodeled, with the three buildings that comprised the business now clearly demarcated along Carson Street. ...

The Silver Spur Casino closed.

1974

Boxing

Yaqui Lopez squared off in the squared circle against Joe Cokes for the light heavyweight championships of three states: Lopez's native California, Cokes's home state of Texas, and Nevada, where the bout was being fought.

Specifically, the 12-round bout was being staged at the second annual Cow Pasture Festival, staged by Sharkey's Casino owner Milos "Sharkey" Begovich and promoted by Bill Dickson. The fight went the distance, and Lopez emerged with a majority decision before a crowd of 2,000.

Lopez would go on to fight five times for world titles, though he was never able to capture a belt. He'd be back in Gardnerville the following year, in 1975, defeating Gary Summerhays of Canada in a 10-round unanimous decision. Cokes, meanwhile, turned out to be on the downside of his career: His loss to Lopez was the first of five in his next seven fights, after which he retired from the ring.

In the only knockout on the Cow Pasture Festival card, Jean "the Basque Bomber" Mateo of Stockton scored a seventh-round stoppage of Tucson's Vincent Medina.

Dining

The Embers at 1407 North Carson Street was under new management, with Cathy and Joe Machado now running the popular restaurant.

The atmosphere was part of the attraction at the Embers, with its comfy padded chairs and low bar, fireplace and low lights.

Education

The Bristlecone Building, the first facility owned by Western Nevada College, opened on the new Carson City campus.

The Bath Street offices of the Nevada Appeal were medical offices as of 2022. *Author photo*

Journalism

The *Nevada Appeal* ended more than two decades in the old brewery building and moved into new offices at 200 Bath Street.

Politics

After three years out of political office, Paul Laxalt jumped back into the fray, vying for the U.S. Senate seat being vacated by retiring incumbent Alan Bible. Laxalt defeated another political legend, Harry Reid, by fewer than 1,000 votes.

Ironically, Reid would succeed him in the Senate after his

13 years in office were up and would go on to become Nevada's longest serving senator, not to mention Senate Majority Leader.

1975

Basketball

Carson High wasn't favored to win the state basketball title at the start of the season, or even at the beginning of the championship tourney.

The team had made the tournament each of the previous two years, but had lost in the first round both times. So most of the attention was focused on Las Vegas, which came into the tourney unbeaten at 25-0, and Clark, which had just two losses on its record — both in overtime to (you guessed it) Vegas.

Carson made some noise by not only making it into the second round for the first time in three years, but doing so with a resounding 71-39 rout of Bishop Gorman. Mike Longero, Carson's 6-foot-4½ forward, dominated on the inside, pulling down 20 rebounds and blocking five shots to go with 15 points.

Only two Gorman players reached double figures against Carson's zone defense.

Still, Gorman coach Tom Motley gave the Senators little chance in their semifinal showdown with Las Vegas. "There's no chance," the Senators could win, he declared. Las Vegas and Clark had "so much talent it's unbelievable. They're stronger than most California teams."

The numbers seemed to back him up. Vegas had advanced to the semis by dismantling Reno 64-35 — the same Reno team that had handed Carson its first loss of the season back in February, 60-58.

The Vegas coach lit a fire under the Senators when he was

quoted as saying the north state teams were so familiar with each other that they played "lunchtime basketball."

But Longero scoffed at his team's underdog status. "The South is saying we play lunchtime basketball up here," he said. "We'll see now."

Everyone did see, because Carson showed them, stunning Vegas in a 60-55 upset in the AAA semifinals that wasn't as close as the final score might indicate. The Senators built a 17-8 advantage after the first quarter, then held off a charge by the Wildcats to lead by one, 24-23, at halftime.

It was then that they turned on the afterburners, scoring the first 14 points of the second half to take a commanding 38-23 lead.

Longero had 17 points to go with 16 rebounds, and Paul Gray added 16 points to pace the Senators.

Vegas was out. Then, it was Clark's turn.

Playing before an overflow crowd of 7,000 fans at Reno's Centennial Coliseum, Carson bolted to a 22-15 lead after the first period, only to see Clark cut the deficit to one at halftime, 36-35. It stayed close the rest of the way, as Longero once again paced the Senators with 21 points and 20 rebounds, while outside marksman Paul Gray added 21 points of his own.

Carson suffered a major blow when Longero fouled out with 1 minute, 25 seconds left and the Senators on top 64-59. But junior guard Jim Salazar hit a pair of free throws a minute later to restore the five-point margin, and a pair of late long-range field goals by Clark proved to be too little, too late.

Salazar finished with 14 points.

Longero described the 68-67 triumph as "a longtime dream come true," and indeed it was. Carson hadn't won a championship since 1938 and hadn't even been to the finals since losing to Rancho 60-51 for the 1961 AA Division title. No team from Northern Nevada had won the title in 12 years.

"There's nothing to compare to it," Gray said. "It's the greatest feeling. It's been a long time for the North."

Education

Douglas High School opened on Highway 88 in Minden.

The Silver Spur became the Lucky Spur in 1975. *Photo by Scott Schrantz*

Gaming

The Silver Spur Casino reopened as the Lucky Spur. But it would only last three years before closing again, this time for good. It would later undergo extensive remodeling to become The Union eatery and taphouse, seen at left (author photo)

Music

T-Car Speedway hosted a pair of holiday concerts in 1975, beginning with a Memorial Day weekend concert on Sunday, May 25 headlined by guitarist Bo Diddley and San Francisco-based funk band Cold Blood, along with Woodstock veteran Country Joe McDonald, rockers Stoneground, and blues guitarist John Lee Hooker.

Labor Day weekend brought two days of music at the speedway.

Blues guitarist Elvin Bishop, whose signature hit, "Fooled Around and Fell in Love," would hit No. 3 on the pop charts a few months later, headlined Sunday's show along with a return engagement by Cold Blood. Also returning to the T-Car stage were Country Joe McDonald and Stoneground, joined by four other acts. Buck Owens and the Buckaroos with Susan Raye had top billing for the holiday show Monday.

Retail

After six years in business, the Disco Discount Department Store came to the same conclusion reached by its predecessor at the Carson Mall, Gray Reid's: It couldn't make a profit there.

In fact, the chain was having problems outside Carson City too. It had grown from a dozen stores in 1969 to 70 in about five years, but plans were announced at the end of 1974 to close 25 of those locations.

In fact, the Carson store had been doing fine: turning a profit until '74. But then things started to sour, and a Disco spokesman said the store was being closed because "the economic climate in retailing is poor throughout the country."

The loss of Disco was a major blow, but the Carson Mall didn't have to wait long for a replacement: In July, J.C. Penney announced plans to replace Disco as the mall's main anchor. It would be the chain's eighth store in Nevada, opening in November, just in time for the holiday season.

District manager Paul Simons told the *Nevada State Journal* he didn't know why Gray Reid's and Disco had failed, but he was confident that the same thing would "definitely not" happen to Penney's — even with imminent competition from a new indoor mall planned up the street.

"I feel there is plenty of room for competition," he said, citing growth in the area and the potential for pulling customers from Minden, Gardnerville, and South Lake Tahoe. "It's a great little town," he said of Carson City. "The people are so darned friendly, and I'm sure they'll all be our customers."

In the long run, however, J.C. Penney wouldn't last in the mall, either. It would relocate to the new Southgate Mall and would be replaced by Fresno-based Gottschalks, which in turn would be replaced by Sportsman's Warehouse.

1976

Cinema

John Wayne's final movie, *The Shootist*, was filmed in the historic district of Carson City. Lauren Bacall, Ron Howard, James Stewart, and Harry Morgan were also in the star-studded cast. The Krebs-Peterson House at 500 Mountain Street in Carson City was specifically used in the film.

Wayne stayed at the Ormsby House during shooting.

He granted an interview in his room there with a reporter from the *Reno Evening Gazette*, who asked him about a director's comment that it could be his last film.

"Bull! It won't be my last film," he thundered.

Unfortunately, he turned out to be wrong.

The Krebs-Peterson house, built in 1914, was used as a location for *The Shootist*, John Wayne's final film. *Author photo*

Dining

If you wanted a souvenir from a brothel without actually going there, you could stop in for a drink or a bite to eat at Dug's West Indies on the north end of town.

Dinner service ran from 5 to midnight, with the house specialty being Polynesian and Chinese food.

The establishment opened an hour earlier, at 4 p.m., for drinks, with the Tiki Bar serving up cocktails with colorful names like Suffering Bastard whose contents were supposedly "too dangerous to print," and the Shark's Tooth, which featured "rum with a whale of a bite." A Great Dane joined patrons, warming himself by the bar's fireplace.

The bar and restaurant were decorated to theme, with tikis, fishing nets, seashells, and anchors, etc. creating the proper atmosphere. If you were a male patron and filled your bladder with booze, you'd have to brave the "shark-infested men's room."

To promote his bar, owner Dug Picking hit on an idea in the mid-1970s to sell souvenir decanters with seagoing themes. ("Captain Dug" himself had sailed the high seas as a fishing boat captain after leaving his native Estonia and before coming to Nevada in 1954.)

In 1976, the Moonlight Ranch six miles east of town commissioned him to create a decanter for the brothel, and Picking sold so many of them that other brothels asked him for their own designs. He wound up producing 47 limited-edition brothel decanters for places like Billie's Day N Night, the Shamrock Ranch, Fran's Ranch, and the Chicken Ranch.

A madam at one Lyon County brothel saddled up to the bar one night and downed five Suffering Bastards, so Picking decided to have a little fun. When she told him to call her a cab, he started pounding away on a Cuban drum he kept at the restaurant, insisting it was his way of summoning the cab.

Incredulous and inebriated, the woman started cussing him out, but he insisted: "This is how we call a cab. We use drums."

The prank worked because Picking had seen a cab pulling into the parking lot before he pulled out the drum. On cue, the taxi driver entered the bar and said, "You called for a cab?"

Picking's friend Gary Evans said the woman was so nonplussed, she downed two more Suffering Bastards and barely made it to the taxi.

Picking retired in 1987, but not before he embarked on a different kind of journey that wound up running aground: the never-completed Windjammer Casino, a gambling complex that was to feature a 345-foot replica of a windjammer with 200-foot-high masts, along with a lighthouse that was designed as a beacon for motorists traveling Highway 50.

But Picking's divorce interrupted the project, and it was ultimately abandoned. He moved to Mexico before returning to Nevada and settling in Las Vegas. ...

Heidi's Family Restaurant, with its distinctive windmill.
Author photo

Heidi's Family Restaurant opened at 1020 North Carson Street. The windmill symbolism on the sign out front wasn't new, though.

The Old Dutch Mill had operated at the same location since 1935. A photo from the following year shows a small windmill-shaped building serving Coca-Cola and Chism Ice Cream, which was made along the Truckee River in Reno.

One visitor recalled visiting the eatery in the early 1940s and ordering a meal that included a burger, chips, and a pickle: all for 15 cents.

By the 1950s, the building had expanded into a full-fledged restaurant with a dining room; the still-large windmill was now protruding from the roof, and it was still advertising Chism Ice Cream. The current building was built around 1962.

In 1986, Heidi's Pancake House owner Don Rosenthal and his business partner Don Thayer bought the restaurant, which was renamed Heidi's Dutch Mill. As locations were added in Minden, Reno, and Fallon, the name was changed again, to Heidi's Family Restaurant.

These days at Heidi's, the big windmill is gone, but the symbol is preserved on a sign on the corner.

Fire

A fire in Kings Canyon west of town turned deadly for three of the five firefighters aboard a helicopter that crashed on their way to battle a nearby fire July 5.

Kings Canyon firefighter tribute. *Author photo*

An unattended campfire apparently sparked the blaze, which burned 40 acres in hard-to-reach terrain. The helicopter crew was called in to battle it, but the Bell Jet Ranger crashed, claiming the lives of Carson City's John Ivins and James Davidson of Nevada City, California.

Kenneth Carvin of Carson City later died of his injuries at Washoe Medical Center.

The other two crew members, however, managed to survive: Peggy Kubly of Iowa and Robert Meredith of Carson were both hospitalized but were reportedly "doing very well" two days after the crash.

Politics

Harold Jacobsen, former chairman of the University of Nevada Board of Regents, defeated Public Works board engineer Joseph Littlefield by 271 votes out of 9,601 cast to become mayor of Carson City.

He would serve as mayor for the next eight years. During his tenure, Carson's growth rate was capped at 3 percent (making it the only county in the state with a growth cap) and planning for the U.S. 395 bypass began.

Retail

It seems one enclosed mall wasn't enough for Carson City, so developers built a second: the Silver City Mall, at the intersection of Carson and Fairview.

That was just a couple of city blocks north of its competitor, an in-your-face challenge to the established mall.

A new Kmart anchored the center, which also included an Albertson's supermarket, Skaggs drugstore, Nevada First Thrift, and Radio Shack. Over the years, tenants included the Bookcellar bookstore, Taqueria Los Tres Amigos, The Gift Box, Silver State Fitness, Sav-On drugs, Animoto Japanese Restaurant, Interstate Insurance, and an oak furniture store.

1977

Dining

A new business opened in a very old house.

The nearly 4,500-square-foot Victorian mansion was built in 1864. It had been home to Judge Michael Murphy in the

1890s and later to Frank Murphy, vice president and general manager of the V&T Railroad in the 1920s.

The house was built beyond what was then the north end of town, but the city gradually caught up to it and that section of Carson Street went from rural and residential to retail/commercial. Carson and William streets, which met nearby, became a pair of U.S. highways (395 and 50, respectively).

The house's character changed with the times, as William Porter set up an antique shop there that later became Bill Porter's Music Box, which boasted an "antique shop, cocktails, quiet atmosphere, nostalgic meals." Browsers were welcome, an ad in the *Nevada Appeal* assured readers, and the place was open every day except Monday as of 1956.

The Music Box was aptly named. In a column for the *Reno Gazette-Journal*, Sue Morrow would later recall Porter playing an organ that he'd set up like a piano bar, adding that friends of his who were also musicians — including Nevada Highway Patrol chief Bob Stenovich — would drop by on weekends for jam sessions.

Another regular, an art teacher at the Stewart Indian School, would sketch caricatures of frequent customers on napkins.

When 1977 rolled around, the place had new owners: Paul and Adele Abowd, who opened Adele's Restaurant there. The building eventually expanded with new wings on both sides and in the back, offering seating for 148 in the café, bar, and on the veranda. The neon sign above the door, retained from the Music Box years, just said BAR, but there was a lot more to be had inside.

Everything was farm to table: "organic, open-range, and humanely raised, as available" on a vast menu of dishes drawn from local growers and ranchers.

The Alpine Ranch supplied pork from Washoe; the Borda Family provided Nevada lamb; beef came from Bently Ranch in Carson Valley; the Glorious Garlic Farm in Washoe supplied potatoes, Japanese winter squash, heirloom pumpkins, and (of course) six kinds of garlic.

This BAR sign, which dates from the Music Box years and was retained at Adele's, was moved to Dayton and is all that's left of the old eatery after a fire destroyed it. Author photo.

Adele's served chicken and duck eggs, rabbits, fresh greens, and veggies from Nancy's Green Barn Farm in Dayton, as well as homemade ice cream from the Hoch Family Creamery in Minden.

All that translated into an award-winning selection of meals.

You could get breakfast items like Basque chorizo links; country-style pork or lamb; omelets with crab, spinach, or bacon; crepes; pancakes; oatmeal; or berries and cream. The lunch menu featured crab cakes, ahi tartare, baked brie, and sashimi (there was even an escargot casserole).

For dinner, you could try duck, blackberry lamb chops,

kale pasta, fried or sautéed ousters, all with a choice of salads. More casual dishes included burgers, pasta dishes, and pizzas. In all, there were more than 100 items on the menu, not to mention a wine cellar.

Chef Charlie Abowd, Paul and Adele's son, did everything from tend bar to wash dishes at the restaurant before he and his wife Karen took over as owners around 1995. It continued to prosper under their leadership, pulling in $1.8 million in gross annual sales.

Unfortunately, a fire in 2018 would shut down the restaurant for good, and the old building was ultimately demolished. The BAR sign was moved to Js' Old Town Bistro in Dayton. ...

The Avitia family opened El Charro Avitia (pictured above in a photo by the author), which was still operating as of 2022. The family had opened the first El Charro three years earlier in Bishop, and another would follow in 1980 in Ridgecrest.

The restaurant has been chosen among the nation's 50 best Hispanic Restaurants by *National Hispanic Magazine* and among the top 100 by *National Restaurant Hospitality Magazine*.

Gaming

Business was booming at Carson City casinos in the spring, raking in $5.7 million in gross revenues for a whopping 41 percent increase over the same quarter the previous year.

Part of this was due to increased business at the Ormsby House, said Jack Stratton, a member of the state's Gaming Control Board. "The Ormsby House is starting to move," he said, citing improvements made by new owner Woody Loftin. "Woody is starting to turn that place around."

But Stratton pointed to another factor, as well: the opening of the Golden Spike Casino in the old Carson Theatre at Carson and Washington streets. The movie house, which opened in 1954 and closed down in the mid-1970s, had found new life as a casino with 150 slot machines, a $25,000 keno operation, six 21 games, and a craps table. There was also a sports book, 80-seat restaurant, and 26-seat bar.

But opening the new casino was anything but easy. The Golden Spike had run into a wall of opposition from the Nugget just down the street, claiming the new casino didn't have enough parking to accommodate the business it would generate.

Ted Stokes, an attorney for the City Center Motel (which, not coincidentally, was controlled by the Nugget's ownership) appealed the decision along with the Downtowner Motel and First National Bank, claiming the Golden Spike wasn't in compliance with the city code's requirements for off-street parking.

"They are concerned the customers of the casino will be filling up their parking areas, which are immediately adjacent to the proposed casino," Stokes said, insisting that the Nugget wasn't worried about competition from the new casino. "Parking is the sole question," he told the Carson Regional Planning Commission.

The Golden Spike's attorney countered that the new business wouldn't require that much parking because much of its business would come from buses and foot traffic from guests at downtown motels. Besides, the cinema at that site had never generated any complaints from the Nugget or anyone else.

The city, threatened with legal action by the Golden Spike, eventually allowed the project to move forward.

Carson River Park, 2022. *Author photo*

Weather

Drought hit western Nevada, with just 42,278 acre-feet of water measured in the Carson River system.

1978

Lodging

Travelodge's latest project was exciting enough to keep even its famous Sleepy Bear mascot awake.

The sleepwalking teddy bear wearing a nightcap, nightshirt, and slippers was set to oversee a new project: a hotel-casino with 96 rooms, 78 slot machines, six blackjack tables, two poker tables, and a craps table. All those lights and slot-machine sounds were bound to keep even the sleepiest bear alert.

The Travelodge hotel-casino was being run by Woody Loftin, who also operated the nearby Ormsby House on Carson Street.

1979

Cinema

The Nevada State Prison, frequently used in films, turned up again in *Flesh and Blood*, with Tom Berenger playing a former convict turned professional boxer.

Cross Country

The Stewart Indian School won the last of seven consecutive state cross country championships.

Fire

The electric clock stood frozen at 11:17.

Forty-three minutes before midnight on March 28. That's when the fire started at the *Nevada Appeal* newspaper offices at 200 Bath St.

The building, just four years old, was 80 percent damaged, with the cost of the blaze estimated at between $300,000 and $500,000, including a quarter-million dollars to the structure alone.

"The whole middle of the building is a total loss," Carson Fire Chief Bernard Sease said, adding that the structure didn't have a sprinkler system. The fire spread quickly through an open attic, though the pressroom was spared by a steel door and fire walls.

But the *Appeal* vowed to rise from the ashes.

Indeed, it didn't miss a beat, publishing a 24-page edition that very day headlined "Fire Guts Appeal, newspaper's operation wrecked" Staffers operated out of editor Sue Morrow's home, the *South Lake Tahoe Tribune*, and a suite at the Frontier Motel. The paper was printed at the *Las Vegas Review-Journal*, which at the time was owned by the same parent company.

The building, once it was refurbished, would be bigger and better than it was before, according to Dave Osborn, the *Appeal*'s general manager. "We had outgrown it," he said, estimating that the new structure would be 25 percent larger than its burned-out predecessor.

Investigators had to sift through debris 2½ feet deep to get to the bottom of the case. But they were sure it was arson. There were signs that the rear door had been forced open, for one thing. And Tom Huddleston, the state's fire marshal, said whoever started the fire probably used cleaning fluid from the newspaper's circulation department to ignite the blaze.

"We know where the accelerant was put down on the floor, how he trailed it all the way down the hallway, which door he went out of and where it was lit," sheriff's detective Joe Curtis later recalled. "But tying it to a person was an impossible task. There were no witnesses, nobody saw vehicles in the area."

Curtis said the investigation focused on a longtime employee who held a lesser position at the newspaper: "We thought we had him, but we could never prove it, for court purposes."

Justice

Jesse Bishop became the last person in Nevada to be executed using poison gas on October 22. The legislature would change the method of execution to lethal injection in 1983.

Prostitution

A grand jury indicted Joe Conforte, owner of the Starlight Ranch in Mound House, on charges of attempting to bribe Lyon County District Attorney John Giomi.

Conforte had been a majority partner in the Starlight with Kitty Bono, taking two-thirds of the profits. But when she demanded a 50-50 split, he refused. She therefore left the partnership and had the Starlight's license transferred to another Mound House brothel.

That left Conforte without a license, and he approached Giomi about helping him obtain one for the Starlight, giving him $1,000 on one occasion and $400 more at another meeting (Giomi, who was cooperating with law enforcement, was not implicated in any crime.)

Prosecutors claimed to have tapes implicating Conforte, but Conforte denied the charges. "I am not going to be convicted because there was no bribery involved," he maintained. "I am 100 percent for legalized prostitution and 100 percent against corruption; and Lyon County is full of it."

Conforte, who was appealing a guilty verdict and 20-year sentence for tax evasion at the time, fled the country in 1980 and spent three years in Brazil. He eventually returned and served one year of his 20-year sentence.

In the Lyon County case, he was sentenced to 18 months in prison, to run concurrently with his tax evasion sentence. He was released from federal prison in 1984 and retired to Brazil in 1991, selling the Mustang Ranch. He is believed to have died in Brazil in 2019.

CARSON CITY CENTURY

Crazy Eighties
1980-1989

The Nevada State Railroad Museum opened in 1980 as the Virginia & Truckee Railroad Museum.
Author photos

1980

Milestones

With a population of 32,022, the state capital had more than doubled in size over just the previous 10 years and was more than six times the size it had been just 20 years earlier.

The Cracker Box diner opened in 1980. *Author photo*

Dining

The Cracker Box opened as a 24-seat diner on May 10 at 402 East William Street, serving breakfast and lunches seven days a week.

Menu items at the diner, which remains open as of this writing, include hand-dipped chicken fried steak, flapjack sandwiches, bagels, sandwiches, salads with dressings made in-house, and homemade soups.

Education

Federal money had run out, and the Stewart Indian School was closing.

"We have no recourse," Administrative Officer Dan Allen told the *Reno Gazette-Journal* on the decision to close the school. "It was nothing we had any control over."

Allen said he'd written a report to the Bureau of Indian Affairs, asking that the school stay open, but that "the decision was made at the Washington level," where orders were given to close the school and "just like in the military, we had to carry them out."

As a result, the students would be sent to other BIA facilities in Riverside, Utah, and Phoenix. The desks, beds, and textbooks would be sent off too, with the school's 68 full-time employees being reassigned or given early retirement. Budget cuts had already led to reduced staffing, with the school having reduced its payroll from 116 full-time employees a year earlier.

"It's a case where Indians have something good going for them, and the white people want it," student Ronnie Bircham wrote in the *Warpath* newspaper on May 15.

Between its founding in 1890 and its ultimate closure 90 years later, an estimated 30,000 students were educated there.

Prostitution

What did local folks in the Mound House area think of the legal brothels operating there?

According to a poll, they were just fine with it.

The *Tri-County Times* and *Mason Valley News* asked readers to send in ballots declaring whether they preferred retaining legalized prostitution or abolishing it in Lyon County.

The results were clear: 527 ballots came back in favor of the brothels, while just 167 were opposed countywide. In the Mound House area, the vote was even more one-sided: 127 ballots supported the brothels, while just 12 opposed them.

Comments from readers included: "Brothels should be closer to our taverns," and "Treat the brothels like an ordinary business and don't give them so much trouble each step of the way."

Transportation

The Nevada State Railroad Museum opened in Carson City as the Virginia & Truckee Railroad Museum.

The idea of a railroad museum in the city had been discussed as far back as 1938, when it was suggested by Graham Hardy of Oakland, president of the Nevada-California Railroad Society. But nothing had come of it, and a plan to display an old V&T caboose on a city sidewalk downtown along Caroline Street 17 years later had also gone awry. The chamber of commerce approved the caboose display, only to reverse course when Shell Oil announced plans to use the area for a new entrance to its service station.

Talks of creating the V&T Railroad Museum had been under way through much of the 1970s, and the project really got rolling in 1979 with a grant of nearly $662,000 from the Fleischmann Foundation to fund the restoration of locomotives and other rolling stock for the museum.

1981

Community

Local train enthusiasts used rail from the Carson & Colorado railroad to create a narrow-gauge railroad over a 1.25-mile course at Mills Park. The new track, designed for families and especially kids, opened on Independence Day.

The Mills Park train and track. *Author photos*

Retail

Wilbur's Men's Shop, a longtime presence in Carson City, declared bankruptcy.

1982

Baseball

Carson High School's quarterback was turning into what the *Reno Evening Gazette* called a "pleasant surprise" on the baseball field.

In his first year starting at third base, the junior turned in a stellar performance during a game in Hawaii, hitting for the cycle (a single, double, triple and home run — a grand slam, at that).

"The best thing about him is he's only a junior," coach Ron McNutt said. "I think he's a real prospect. He's got all the tools. We knew he'd be strong defensively, but he's really shown us something with his power."

He finished the season as the team's leading hitter, batting .500 in conference games, and was named co-Northern AAA player of the year. But that was just the beginning of his success: In three seasons playing shortstop at the University of Nevada-Las Vegas, he hit .327 with 58 home runs and 217 runs batted in.

After that, he was drafted by the San Francisco Giants and began a Major League career that spanned 17 seasons with the Giants, Cleveland Indians, and Arizona Diamondbacks.

A five-time all-star, Matt Williams led the National League in RBI with 122 in 1990 and in home runs with 43 in 1994. He finished his career with a .268 lifetime batting average, 378 home runs and 1,218 RBI.

Cinema

Set masters transformed the Brewery Arts Center into a nightclub for *Honkytonk Man*, starring Clint Eastwood as a country singer dying of tuberculosis. Eastwood's son Kyle also starred in the film, which included street scenes shot in Dayton and a scene with a bull filmed in Fallon.

Gaming

The Adams brothers added a second story to the Carson Nugget casino, expanding it to 80,000 square feet.

1983

Weather

The Carson City river system was bulging with 825,323 acre-feet of water. That was almost 20 times the amount of water in the system during the drought year of 1977.

1985

Gaming

The Golden Spike, which had opened with such fanfare less than a decade earlier, had a stake driven through its heart by the Nevada State Bank.

The bank foreclosed on the property in mid-November, leaving 120 people without jobs. A sign on the casino doors read "Closed — Please Do Not Come In."

Bank President Richard Carlson said the decision came down to dollars and cents: "We are in the banking business, not the casino business," he told the *Reno Gazette-Journal*. "Business was extremely slow. It's tough to start a new little casino in a small community. Business just wasn't coming in fast enough."

The casino, he said, was never able to catch up with its bills.

Owner J.R. "Spike" Jamison owed the bank a $1 million loan he hadn't been able to repay. He'd filed for Chapter 11 bankruptcy protection in April, but it wasn't enough to save the casino from foreclosure.

"It's been a long battle, and it's not a good day today," he told the *Gazette-Journal* from inside the casino after it closed. "But don't make it sound like a funeral. As soon as I leave, I'm going to put the last chain on the door. I can't even remember what I did before this."

The foreclosure sale produced no bids high enough to pay off the $1 million loan, so the bank took possession of the casino.

Said Carlson: "We just want to go ahead and sell it."

Justice

Carroll Edward Cole became the first person executed in Nevada by lethal injection on December 6.

1986

Dining

John Hurzel opened Carson City's second Scotty's restaurant at 2811 South Carson Street. He and his brother and sister already owned the first Scotty's (which would later become Living the Good Life) up the road when he purchased the new place from Denny's.

The national chain had operated it for a couple of years; it had been open for about five years as VIPs — part of a now-defunct Oregon-based chain — before that.

"This was the end of town then," Hurzel told the *Nevada Appeal* in 2017, when the restaurant was closing. "There were no car dealers. The end of the frontage road was the end of town."

The location was perfect to attract visitors driving into town from the south, but the business got off to a rocky start when a fire started in the deep fryer, leaving the restaurant with smoke and water damage. The insurance wasn't enough to pay for repairs, so the family sold the first Scotty's to a new owner to cover the cost.

That owner kept the Scotty's name, so Hurzel and his siblings changed the name of his new place to Grandma Hattie's in honor of their mom.

To emphasize that it was a family restaurant, they converted the bar that had been there into a meeting area that hosted groups such as the Lions and Toastmasters over the years.

The restaurant featured an extensive menu that included items like meatloaf; liver, bacon, and onions; huevos rancheros; potato pancakes; chicken and mushrooms; and sliders dubbed "buddies." Desserts included Papa John's Bread Pudding, and the D.J. Twinkie Treat (a Twinkie cake covered with ice cream and chocolate sauce).

1988

Politics

Marv Teixeira was elected mayor of Carson City with 53 percent of the vote. Teixeira would serve two terms as mayor, retiring in 1996, but would later return for a third term in 2005.

A youth sports coach who worked to develop the Boys and Girls Clubs of Western Nevada, Teixeira worked to persuade the legislature to move Nevada Day celebrations to the weekend, instead of having them fall on the actual anniversary of Nevada statehood. He also helped create the Carson Booster Club.

Teixeira was instrumental in efforts to reconstruct the Virginia & Truckee Railroad. By 2022, a reconstructed portion of the railroad ran between Virginia City and Gold Hill.

1989

Cinema

Tom Selleck played *An Innocent Man* framed by corrupt police officers who's out for revenge when he's paroled from prison in this movie, much of which was shot at the Nevada State Prison. Inmates were paid $1 a day to serve as extras for the film, and an extra guard tower (in author photo, right) was added for effect. Selleck would donate money to upgrade the prison's basketball court.

Meanwhile, Clint Eastwood returned to Carson City to film *Pink Cadillac* with Bernadette Peters. Some filming was done at Fuji Park.

Play On
1990-1999

Gold Dust West was built as Piñon Plaza near the future site of the 395 interstate bypass. *Author photo*

1990

Cinema
James Caan was in *Misery* in this adaptation of a Stephen King novel about an author held hostage by an obsessed fan, played by Kathy Bates. Some filming was done on Clear Creek Road, old U.S. 50 in Carson City.

Milestones
More than 40,000 people (40,443 to be exact) called Carson City home at the dawn of the new decade, marking a 26.3 percent increase in population. That number would grow

by nearly 30 percent more in the 10 years that followed, hitting 52,547 by the year 2000.

The Silver City Mall was in decline by the 1990s. *Photo by Scott Schrantz*

Retail

J.C. Penney left the Carson Mall for the Southgate Mall to the south, which also boasted Walmart as an anchor tenant.

The departure was part of an exodus of major retailers from the city's two enclosed malls that would hit one hard and spell the beginning of the end for the other.

Silver City Mall would lose its biggest-name tenant, Kmart, which built a new Super K in 1994, and Albertson's left as well. Two new anchor tenants moved in: Office Depot and Ernst, a hardware store that occupied the spot Kmart had vacated.

But Ernst closed in 1996.

Four years later, it was announced that the mall would be demolished and a Lowe's home improvement store would be built on the site.

The Super K, which included a grocery section, wasn't far behind. It was the biggest store in town when it opened, but it closed after just nine years, its parent company fast losing ground to dominant Walmart.

Super Kmart was a big deal. Until it wasn't. *Photo by Scott Schrantz*

1991

Prostitution

The Mustang Ranch meets Disneyland?

Or maybe Westworld without the robots.

That was the germ of an idea floated by William Mace Knapp, a 48-year-old psychologist at Nevada State Prison who was no longer employed there when the prison got wind of his plans. Knapp even had inmates type mailing labels and stuff envelopes with fliers promoting the brothel idea and offering discount coupons.

His wife Pegg, who was warden of the women's facility there, lost her job too. The prison system had a policy against employees holding second jobs in bars, casinos, or other businesses that might be patronized by former offenders.

"It's basically a conflict of interest, said state prison director Ron Angelone. "We're not making a moral judgment. But our missions and goals are in total conflict with the principles that his corporation was talking about."

Knapp's plan, described in the *Mason Valley News*, involved buying the Moonlight Ranch in Mound House and "expanding the facilities' legal license to open a 20-acre western-style park with a genuine house of ill repute on its premises."

Knapp's plans for the "world's first fantasy sex resort" walked a weird tightrope between adult and more conventional entertainment, the sort of place he said you could bring your in-laws. (Yes, he really said that, although he did protest that "we're not talking about Disneyland.")

The Bonanza Mining Camp would have a gold mine, general store, gunfights, burro rides, and a dance hall complete with working prostitutes clad "like Miss Kitty in Gunsmoke." You wouldn't be able to have sex in the Hoist Works Saloon, though. You'd have to take a stagecoach or hoof it to the Shaft House, Knapp's name for the proposed brothel, to go the full monty.

"We always came here on vacation, and after hearing so much about the brothels, we drove by to see what they looked like," Knapp said. "They didn't look very exciting. We wondered how come nobody has tried to do a nice Victorian Wild West-type building like you'd see in the movies?"

For their part, the folks at the Moonlight Ranch weren't too interested in Knapp's grandiose plans.

"We're all laughing at this guy," the manager said. "He keeps talking about getting prostitution out of the back alleys, but that's where everybody wants it — the state, the county, the residents and even the customers."

Knapp's idea never came to fruition, and he was still out of a job at the prison. In 1995, however, the Nevada Supreme Court overruled a Carson City District Court judge and ruled that Knapp should be rehired.

Transportation

A listing on the National Register of Historic Places wasn't enough to save the Virginia & Truckee Railroad Engine House and Shops from the wrecking ball.

Carson City founder Abraham Curry had started work on the roundhouse in November of 1882 and completed construction the following July. The complex eventually also included a foundry, water works, and engine room, along with car, tin, smith, pattern, and machine shops.

Stephen Drew, curator of the California State Railroad Museum, called the complex "one of Carson City's most significant and longstanding architectural features." But because it was on private land and deemed an "unsafe hazard," the city was unable to halt its demolition.

Owner Paul Larquier, a California resident, ordered it torn down. The Larquier family had owned the complex since Larquier's father purchased it in 1955.

1992

Prostitution

Dennis Hof purchased and renovated the old Moonlight Ranch, now known as the Moonlite BunnyRanch. Hof would eventually buy the other three brothels in Mound House as well: Kitty's Guest House (which he renamed BunnyRanch II and, later, Love Ranch), the Kit Kat, and the Sagebrush.

Dennis Hof purchased the Moonlite BunnyRanch in 1992. He eventually bought the other three brothels in Mound House as well. *Author photo*

The Moonlite BunnyRanch is on the north side of U.S. 50 heading east from Carson City, while the other three are clustered in the Mound House "red light district" on the other side of the road a little farther east.

Hof also owned two other brothels in Pahrump, Nye County.

He would enter the political arena in 2018 as a Republican candidate for the state Assembly, patterning himself after then-President Donald Trump and styling himself as the "Trump from Pahrump." He won the seat, but was elected posthumously, as the vote came less than a month after his death at age 72.

He died of a heart attack following his birthday party, and his body was found by friend and adult film star Ron Jeremy.

1993

Cinema

The State Capitol and other sites in Carson City were featured in *Sworn to Vengeance*, starring Robert Conrad.

The Marv Teixeira Pavilion at Mills Park started out as the Pony Express Pavilion. *Author photo*

Community

The Pony Express Pavilion opened in Mills Park on U.S. Highway 50. The venue, later renamed Marv Teixeira Pavilion in honor of the city's mayor from 1989 to 1996, was designed to host special events, concerts, and, in winter, ice skating.

It opened in conjunction with an annual event re-creating the Pony Express ride from St. Joseph, Missouri, to Sacramento.

Lodging

The St. Charles Hotel had come full circle. After operating under half a dozen different names since it was built back in 1862, it was once again the St. Charles.

Against all odds, it had outlasted competitors from the first half of the 20th century such as the Arlington and the Ormsby House, and now Carson City businessman Bob McFadden had invested a cool million in the place: $750,000 to buy it and $250,000 more for renovations.

Crooner Tony Bennett ("I Left My Heart in San Francisco") appeared at the opening of Joe Garlic's, as the hotel's new restaurant was called.

McFadden would own the hotel until 2001.

In 2016, a public pedestrian area called McFadden Plaza (below, author photos) would replace Third Street between Carson and Curry.

1994

Community

The Children's Museum of Northern Nevada opened in the old Civic Auditorium on Carson Street, offering hands-on exhibits for children in the arts, sciences, and humanities.

The museum used federal and state grants to replace the roof, renovate the building's interior, and add an elevator.

Fire

Fire Station 1 (above, author photo) moved to 777 South Stewart Street.

Prostitution

A judge dismissed a class-action lawsuit seeking to close Lyon County's four legal brothels.

Judge David Gamble ruled that granting, revoking, denying, or suspending licenses to run a legal house of prostitution was "a discretionary function of the board of county commissioners."

The Skate Trak skating rink was converted into a Goodwill store. *Author photo*

Recreation

Construction began in the fall on the Skate Trak skating rink, built along Highway 50 heading east toward Virginia City. The nearly 31,000-square-foot facility housed a large rink that measured 100 by 210 feet, with a DJ booth up top, and looked more like a car dealership than a skating center.

The roller rink wasn't just a business, but a personal passion for owners Pam and Rick Tierney, whose own kids were serious speedskaters.

They opened Skate Trak, Pam Tierney told the *Reno Gazette-Journal*, when she and her husband realized that their family was "living the sport — we were involved in it seven days a week."

Their 17-year-old daughter, Jennifer, and 14-year-old son, Todd (then an eighth-grader at Carson Middle School), both qualified for the indoor nationals event at Syracuse in 1995.

Todd won a pair of bronze medals.

"It's a family thing," Pam Tierney said of the business. "Todd floorguards the rink and Jen is a full-time disc jockey for us. I just kind of fell into being the coach and the whistleblower."

Skate Trak hosted events such as Family Skate Night for Advocates to End Domestic Violence on their yellow oval rink. A couple of hours each morning were dedicated to mothers with youngsters in strollers, and the rink also offered programs for beginning skaters and a Christian Music Night.

In March of 1996, the Tierneys brought together more than 500 Junior Olympians and U.S. Confederation of Amateur Roller Skaters competitors for an inline skating event. Teams from as far away as Sacramento, Las Vegas, Riverside, and Modesto competed.

The rink eventually closed and became a Goodwill store.

1995

Cinema

Some scenes from *Showgirls*, a movie about an ambitious Las Vegas dancer (Elizabeth Berkley), were filmed in Carson City. So were scenes from *Trail of Tears*, a television movie starring Katy Sagal and Pam Dawber as two women trying to free their kidnapped children.

Dining

Dining choices in Carson City included the Buffalo Club, featuring dishes such as Cajun chicken Caesar salad, pasta, steaks and chops, at 2729 North Carson Street.

Other Carson Street eateries serving American fare were Flapjack's Vittles at 306 South Carson, Grandma Hattie's at

2811 South Carson, Scotty's Family Restaurant at 1480 North Carson, and Stanley's at 4239 North Carson.

The Cracker Box was open out on U.S. 50 East, and you could travel a little farther out to visit Thurman's Ranch House.

There were six Chinese restaurants in town, and two Japanese restaurants (Yamacho on North Carson and Amimoto on Fairview). Gourmet-to-go international food could be had at the Wild Scallion at 318 North Carson, which also offered espresso, catering and homemade desserts.

For Italian fare, Valentino's was at 2729 North Carson, Garibaldi's had recently opened on Carson just north of Proctor, and there were half a dozen pizza places from which to choose. Seven Mexican restaurants were open, with names like Tito's on William Street, Los Tres Amigos on Roop, El Charro Avitia and Tequila Dan's on South Carson, and MiCasa Too on North Carson.

Casino dining was another option. The new Piñon Plaza (see below) offered a "Southwest Super Buffet with Mongolian grills" known for offering "huge varieties of fresh, homecooked foods served for peanuts."

Gaming

Carson Street wasn't the only place major casinos could be found in Carson City.

Not anymore.

Clark Russell, owner of the Carson Station Casino (now the Max Casino) downtown was staking some of his chips on a new casino in a new location: the Southwest-themed Piñon Plaza out on U.S. 50 at Lompa Lane.

Future plans for the U.S. 395 bypass — a section of current Interstate 580 that was ultimately completed in stages between 2006 and 2017 — made the location even more appealing to Russell.

"I felt this was a good location because of the growth in the city and U.S. 50 out to Lyon County," Russell told the Reno Gazette-Journal. "And sooner or later there's going to be a freeway there, and we'll be right next to it."

If you didn't win at the slot machine, you could take your frustrations out by hurling a 15-pound ball at 10 white pins on one of the casino's 32 bowling lanes. The 29,000-square-foot bowling center was the first in the United States to feature Frameworx bowling equipment from Brunswick.

Russell's project, which would get a new identity a decade later as Gold Dust West, was set to include a 100-room hotel, 30,000-square-foot casino with 350 slot machines, an RV park with space for 77 vehicles, two restaurants, a sports book, and a sports bar.

The complex was to be built in three phases, with the $9 million first phase including the casino, restaurant, and bowling center …

Barry Silverton used a $5.5 million loan to buy and reopen the Ormsby House. Future Reno Mayor Bob Cashell served as manager for the property under Silverton, and it turned a profit for the first time since its days under Woody Loftin, but the good fortune wouldn't last.

1996

Community

Blame it on the pigeon poop.

Seriously, that's what they did: Pigeon droppings that had built up over the years was blamed for the partial collapse of the shuttered Golden Spike Casino's marquee when it came crashing down on the sidewalk below.

Fortunately, no one was hurt.

But the *Reno Gazette-Journal* left no doubt that the culprit was "years of pigeon poop."

The new city hall was installed in a former Bank of America building on Carson Street. *Author photo*

Government

The city purchased a former Bank of America building at Carson and Musser, then spent more than $600,000 to remodel it and transform it into a new city hall. The new design featured a red-brick front and arched windows designed to replicate the design of the demolished V&T roundhouse.

Politics

Ray Masayko, a retired utility employee, was elected mayor of Carson City, defeating Patt Quinn-Davis by 400 votes. Masayko, a lifelong Democrat, drew notice when he switched his party affiliation to Republican four months before the election.

Though the office of mayor was nominally nonpartisan, Carson City was a GOP stronghold. Masayko said he switched parties before deciding to run for office, so the change wasn't driven by a desire to enhance his appeal in heavily Republican Carson City. But Quinn-Davis said flatly, "I don't believe him."

Masayko would be re-elected in 2000.

1997

Gaming

With Piñon Plaza firmly established out on U.S. 50, it was only a matter of time — and not very much of it — before another casino opened in the vicinity.

That casino turned out to be Slot World, which focused strictly on slot machines to the exclusion of other casino staples such as poker, roulette, and 21.

The Slot World Casino opened near U.S. 50 in 1997. *Author photo*

1998

Cinema

Ironwood Stadium Cinema opened in Minden.

Gaming

The Ormsby House closed again when Barry Silverton defaulted on his loan and the property was foreclosed. Don Lehr and Al Fiegehen bought the hotel-casino in 1999 and announced it would undergo extensive renovations, but they ran into a number of hurdles as plans were altered, permits held up, and construction was delayed.

The property remained closed as of 2022.

1999

Fire

The Hunter's Lodge at the southwest corner of Carson and Fourth streets was demolished after being damaged in a fire that started next door.

The Carson City Mint Building, now home to the Nevada State Museum. *Author photo*

References

"50 years ago: Carson City rallies after hospital fire," nevadaappeal.com, Aug. 25, 2018.
"About Sharkey's Casino," sharkeyscasino.com.
Adler, Lee. "Carson Disco to close," Reno Evening Gazette, p. 1, Feb. 10, 1975.
Adler, Lee. "Golden Spike proposal at standstill," Reno Evening Gazette, p. 8, Jan. 29, 1976.
Adler, Lee. "Stewart Indian School padlocked," Reno Gazette-Journal, p. 15, Sept. 30, 1980.
Adler, Lee and Volek, Sue. "Arson probed in Carson newspaper fire," Reno Evening Gazette, p. 1, March 29, 1979.
"Admission Day Festivities At Nevada Capital Draw Crowd of Many Thousands," Reno Evening Gazette, p. 1, Oct. 31, 1938.
"Airport Authority & Staff," flycarsoncity.com.
"All Patients Are Evacuated," Reno Evening Gazette, p. 1, Aug. 26, 1968.
"Archives & College History: History of the College," libguides.tmcc.edu.
"Arlan Robinson," motorsportmemorial.org.
"Arlington Hotel," carsonpedia.com.
"Bank Building Sold in Carson," Reno Evening Gazette, p. 19, March 5, 1959.
"Bankruptcies," Reno Evening Gazette, p. 32, Aug. 13, 1981.
"The Bell in Place," Carson City Daily Appeal, p. 3, March 25, 1906.
Bennett, Ron. "A Point to Prove," Reno Evening Gazette, p. 17, March 7, 1975.

Bennett, Ron. "Carson's Longero: 'It's a lifetime dream come true,'" Reno Evening Gazette, p. 14, March 10, 1975.
Bennett, Ron. "McDougal: 'Lunch time basketball foolish,'" Reno Evening Gazette, p. 8, March 8, 1975.
Benson, Frank. "Senators have fun in Hawaii," Reno Evening Gazette, p. 2D, April 13, 1982.
Boxoffice, June 1, 1959.
"Brief history of the Nevada Appeal," recordcourier.com, March 2, 2005.
Broderick's ad, Nevada State Journal, p. 8, Oct. 25, 1938.
"Brothel History & Background," nevadabrothelassociation.com.
Bubb, Daniel K. "Landing in Las Vegas," University of Nevada Press, June 2012.
Buergin, Miles. "Knowing Nevada: A casino inside the Nevada State Prison," mynews4.com, Sept. 21, 2018.
"Café at Adele's Farm to Table," adelesrestaruantandlounge.com.
Cafferata, Patty. "Capital Punishment Nevada Style," Nevada Lawyer Magazine, June 2010.
"The Capital City Players," Carson City Daily Appeal, p. 1, June 28, 1907.
"Carson City Briefs," Reno Evening Gazette, p. 10, Nov. 29, 1921.
"Carson City Fire Department History," carson.org.
"The Carson City Kid," imdb.com.
"Carson City," nevadaweb.com (archived).
"Carson City Railroad Association," carson.org.
Carson City restaurant guide, Reno Gazette-Journal, Sierra Dining, p. 22, Nov. 19, 1995.
"Carson City's Grandma Hattie's Closing on Wednesday," nevadaappeal.com, Sept. 12, 2017.
"Carson City Shop Area," virginiaandtruckee.com.
"Carson City Social Notes," Nevada State Journal, p. 6, Jan. 11, 1946.
"Carson City Social Notes," Nevada State Journal, p. 11, April 30, 1954.
"Carson Disco Opening Brings Customers from Five Counties," Nevada State Journal, p. 14, Dec. 4, 1969.
Carson Exchange ad, Yerington Times, p. 3, Nov. 23, 1872.
Carson Exchange ad, Carson City Daily Appeal, p. 2, July 26, 1906.
"Carson Fire Loss Exceeds $200,000," Nevada State Journal, p. 12, Jan. 3, 1950.
Carson Horseshoe Club ad
"Carson Is Booming," Nevada State Journal, p. 3, March 9, 1906.
"Carson land purchased for 'top of line' hotel," Reno Evening Gazette, p. 31, May 5, 1978.
"Carson Mayor Defeated in Election Bid," Reno Evening Gazette, p. 11, June 4, 1963.
"Carson Merchants Oppose Casino," Nevada State Journal, p. 25, Jan. 16, 1976.
"Carson Newspaper Makes Survey Of Rent Rates Charged in Motels," Nevada State Journal, p. 3, July 26, 1947.
"Carson officials hear message in mayoral race," Reno Gazette-Journal, p. 1, Nov. 7, 1996.
"Carson-Ormsby Filing Closes With Three in Race for Mayor," Reno Evening Gazette, p. 13, April 21, 1969.
"Carson Rejects Government Split By 2 to 1 Count," Reno Evening Gazette, p, 11, May 2, 1961.
"Carson River Watershed Timeline," cwsd.org.
"Carson Schools List Honor Rolls," Nevada State Journal, p. 2, April 9, 1931.
"Carson Street To Be Closed," Reno Evening Journal, p. 20, Oct. 19, 1954.
Carson Theatre ad for *The Chief*, Reno Gazette, p. 2, Dec. 25, 1933.
"Carson Valley News Briefs," Reno Evening Gazette, p. 10, April 3, 1923.

"The Casino," nevadastateprison.org.
Cassinari, Andi. "Someone 2 Know: Charlie Abowd," 2news.com, March 1, 2018.
"Chaney Kelley trio ending Horseshoe's era," nnbw.com, Nov. 18, 2015.
"Chicken Every Sunday," imdb.com.
"Chill out at Walley's Hot Springs Resort," nevadaappeal.com, March 16, 2017.
Cinematreasures.org.
City Center Motel ad, Nevada State Journal, p. 21, June 16, 1966.
Classified ad: Rex Theater for sale, Nevada State Journal, p. 7, March 21, 1924.
Clodjeaux, Denise. "Iconic Café at Adele's sign stays in family, finds new home at Js' Old Town Bistro in Dayton," carsonnow.org, Dec. 3, 2019.
Cobb, Ty. "Inside Stuff," Nevada State Journal, p. 6, May 10, 1938.
"Community College sets deadline for enrollment," Reno Evening Gazette, p. 21, Aug. 26, 1971.
"The Complete Official Road Guide of the Lincoln Highway," Lincoln Highway Association, 1916.
Conforte, Joe and Toll, David W. "Breaks, Brains, and Balls," Gold Hill Publishing Co., Virginia City, 2011.
"Conforte parole hearing Oct. 8," Mason Valley News, Sept. 28, 1984.
Corona, Marcella and Hagar, Ray. "Celebrate Northern Nevada's famous Awful on National Hamburger Day," rgj.com, May 28, 2019.
Cox, Kate. "The Feds Once Arrested A Rooster Statue Made Out Of Solid Gold," consumerist.com, June 14, 2017.
Cracker Box menu, thecrackerboxdiner.com.
"Crash Claims Third Victim," Nevada State Journal, p. 10, July 8, 1976.
Crawford, Mark. "Carson newspaper fire probe 'plugging along' one year later," Reno Evening Gazette, p. 53, March 28, 1980.
"Dedicated to Carson's Chinese history," recordcourier.com, Sept. 25, 2003.
"Disco to open Carson store," Reno Evening Gazette, p. 8, Oct. 15, 1969.
"Divergent Views on Gambling Act Expressed at Meeting," Reno Evening Gazette, p. 2, Jan. 8, 1931.
"Domestic violence: Thanks to Skate Trak," Reno Gazette-Journal, p. 9, July 8, 1996.
Dornan, Geoff. "Carson City fountain flowing again," apnews.com, Nov. 3, 2016.
"Dorothy's Auto Court," whnpc.com.
Dorson, Jill R. "Nevada Sports Betting Traces Roots To Prison," usbets.com, May 9, 2019.
"Douglas County is Victorious," Reno Evening Gazette, p. 6, March 15, 1915.
Dreiling, Dick. "Last Chance Joe History," sparksmuseum.org.
Drew, Stephen E. "V&T Historical Narrative," ntrrhs.org.
"Early Nevada Family Member Dies in Reno," Reno Evening Gazette, p. 11, May 18, 1959.Embers ad, Reno Evening Gazette, p. 9, June 17, 1974.
Enrico's ad, Reno Evening Gazette, p. 2, May 19, 1956.
"Fire Destroys Six Cabins," Salt Lake Tribune, p. 9, April 23, 1944.
"Fire Fails To Halt Newspaper," Durham (N.C.) Herald-Sun, p. 35, March 30, 1979.
"Five Special Events Set For Remaining Sox Games," Reno Evening Gazette, p. 34, Aug. 27, 1959.
"Flour Mill," bentlyheritage.com.
"Former Carson mayor, 96, dies," nevadaappeal.com, Dec. 17, 2008.
"Former Carson mayor Harold Jacobsen dies," nevadaappeal.com, Feb. 9, 2021.
"Former Carson mayor Marv Teixeira dies," nevadaappeal.com, June 7, 2014.

Frank, George. "Fire Razes Carson City Hospital," Nevada State Journal, p. 1, Aug. 27, 1968.
"Freshmen Gets the Short End," Nevada State Journal, p. 1, Feb. 25, 1911.
"Gambling Bill Defeated by Senate Wednesday," Mason Valley News, p. 1, March 19, 1927.
"Gaming License Bid," Nevada State Journal, p. 31, June 16, 1976.
"Gardnerville and Minden News," Reno Evening Gazette, p. 10, Oct. 2, 1923.
"Gardnerville Hotelmen are Freed by Court," Reno Evening Gazette, p. 8, March 8, 1921.
"Gardnerville, Nevada," nvdnp.wordpress.com.
"Gardnerville Trade Large," Reno Evening Gazette, p. 10, March 28, 1914.
"Grandma Hattie's," menupix.com.
"Gray-Reid's – Nevada's Fine Store," bigmallrat.blogspot.com, July 6, 2011.
"Gray-Reid's Opens Carson Mall Store," Reno Evening Gazette, p. 10, March 17, 1966.
Gray-Reid's photo, Nevada State Journal, p. 8, March 18, 1966.
"Ground Being Prepared For Introduction Soon of Wide Open Gambling Bill," Reno Evening Gazette, p. 2, Feb. 23, 1927.
Gunkel, Terri. "Carson seeded No. 1 in AAA zone baseball," Reno Evening Gazette, p. 3B, May 5, 1982.
Henley, David C. "First Nevada flight made at Carson in 1910," nevadaappeal.com, Oct. 17, 2010.
Herr, Allen and Kathe. "Ragwings Over The Sacramento River," Stansbury Publishing, 2020.
"The history of the Nevada state flag," nevadaappeal.com, Oct. 23, 2014.
Honig-Bear, Sharon. "Derailed Eatery," ediblerenotahoe.com, Spring 2020.
"Honkytonk Man," imdb.com.
"Horses gather at the refurbished watering fountain during Nevada Day Parade," carsonnow.org, Oct. 31, 2016.
"Hotel Business Is Talk Subject," Nevada State Journal, p. 7, April 11, 1940.
"'I feel the history': Stewart Indian School converted into museum to remember dark past," rgj.com, Jan. 24, 2020.
"In Memoriam: Thomas C. Wilson," Nevada Historical Society Quarterly, Fall 1985.
"Indians Beat U.N.," Tonopah Daily Bonanza, p. 4, Nov. 1, 1916.
"Indians Win Championship," Carson City Daily Appeal, p. 1, Nov. 27, 1916.
"J.C. Penney Confirms Carson Store," Nevada State Journal, p. 21, July 17, 1975.
"Jacobsen elected Carson mayor," Reno Gazette-Journal, p. 5, Nov. 3, 1976.
"James J. Corbett vs. Bob Fitzsimmons," boxrec.com.
Jones, Janet. "Haunted Carson City," Arcadia Publishing, 2012.
Jones, Lisa and Sylvain, Diane. "Heard Around the West," hcn.org, Jan. 22, 1996.
"Kidnappers of Son Contacted Sinatra Sr. at Carson Station," Reno Evening Gazette, p. 1, Dec. 11, 1963.
"Kit Carson Stands Here," Reno Evening Gazette, p. 35, April 17, 1959.
"Kovacs Wins Net Battle at Carson," Nevada State Journal, p. 4, May 16, 1938.
Kranc, Lauren. "The True Story of the 1963 Kidnapping of Frank Sinatra Jr.," esquire.com, July 27, 2021.
"Lamb's Impressions," Reno Evening Gazette, p. 3, May 22, 1903.
"Largest Cities in US by Area 2022," worldpopulationreview.com.
Lincoln Highway Association. "The Complete Official Road Guide of the Lincoln Highway," Princeton University, 1916.
"The Lincoln Highway in Nevada," lincolnhighwayassoc.org.

CARSON CITY CENTURY

"Lincoln Victor in Nevada Race," Motor West, p. 22, July 15, 1921.
"Lyon board licenses four brothels," Reno Evening Gazette, April 15, 1972.
Manning, Helen. "Nevada's Story," Reno Gazette-Journal, p. 38, March 1, 1982.
McMillan, Doug. "Fire damages Carson newspaper," Reno Evening Gazette, p. 22, March 29, 1979.
"Medicine Show is Scheduled Admission Day," Nevada State Journal, p. 10, Oct. 27, 1938.
Melton, Rollan. "A gift to Nevadans," Reno Evening Gazette, p. 21, Nov. 28, 1979.
"Memory of V&T Roundhouse isn't fading away," "nevadaappeal.com, July 22, 2017.
Mendoza, Monica. "3 new businesses expected in Carson City's Southgate Mall," Reno Gazette-Journal, Carson-Douglas edition, p. 2, Aug. 13, 1994.
"Millennium Countdown: 1910," recordcourier.com., Dec. 20, 2001.
"Minden Flour Milling Company," carsonpedia.com.
"Minden, Nevada," townofminden.com.
"Minden Notes," Reno Evening Gazette, p. 6, Feb. 28, 1921.
"Mines & Mining History," visitvirginiacitynv.com.
"Mircovich, Andriza," nevadaculture.org (archived).
Montero, David. "Must Reads: Nevada's monopoly on vice may be easing with push to eliminate nearly half the state's brothels," latimes.com, May 6, 2018.
"Moreno, Robert. "A Short History of Carson City," University of Nevada Press, 2011.
Morrow, Sue. "As the capital city grows up, many recall its small-town charm," Carson Times, p. 4, July 21, 2006.
Morrow, Sue. "Dug's West Indies restaurant: It may be gone but not forgotten," Carson Times, p. 4, Sept. 1, 2006.
"Mrs. De Jarlis, Carson Resident Since 1905, Dies," Nevada State Journal, p. 8, Dec. 7, 1932.
Munson, Jeff. "Carson City shuts down Frontier Motel on North Carson, occupants to be vacated by Thursday," carsonnow.org, April 14, 2022.
Myers, Dennis. "Dueling highways," Reno News & Review, April 30, 2015.
Namioka, Jim. "Carson's Old Globe to get new look," Reno Gazette-Journal, p 1, Aug. 1, 1996.
Namioka, Jim. "New Casino in fast lane to opening," Reno Gazette-Journal, p. B1, May 8, 1995.
Nash, Vicki. "Western Nevada community college gets facilities in Carson City," Reno Evening Gazette, p. 27, June 23, 1971.
"The Nevada Burger That Will Make You Feel Like You Can Take On Anything," onlyinyourstate.com, Nov. 19, 2018.
"Nevada casinos increase business over last year," Twin Falls (Idaho) Times-News, p. 16, Aug. 9, 1977.
"Nevada City Pilot Among Dead in Fire-Fighter Crash," The Sacramento Bee, p. 9, July 6, 1976.
"Nevada Day," onlinenevada.org.
"Nevada Decision," Western Highways Builder, p. 19, Dec. 20, 1919.
"Nevada Hymn Sung By 1,000," Nevada State Journal, p. 10, Oct. 26, 1938.
"Nevada's six-weeks divorce law," Mason Valley News, sec. 2., p. 6, March 20, 1981.
"Nevada State Prison – CLOSED," doc.nv.gov (archived).
"New Carson casino proponents face battle with established clubs," Reno Evening Gazette, p. 9, Jan. 21, 1976.
"A New Minor League, the 1907 Nevada State League," minorleagueresearcher.blogspot.com, Nov. 10, 2005.
"The New School," Carson City Daily Appeal, p. 3, May 7, 1906.

New Year's Eve ads, Reno Evening Gazette, p. 8, Dec. 30, 1936.
"Newspaper 'not stilled' by huge fire," nevadaappeal.com, March 23, 2004.
Nicoletta, Julie. "Minden Flour Milling Company," sah-archipedia.org.
"No One to Shoot Murderer," New York Times, Aug. 12, 1912.
"Old Fire Station No. 1," carsonpedia.com.
"Ormsby House in Carson City has a new buyer," nevadaappeal.com, Oct. 29, 2020.
Papinchak, Steve. "Teixeira elected Carson mayor; tax increase defeated,"
    Reno Gazette-Journal, p. 5, Nov. 9, 1988.
"Past Pages for April 30 to May 3, 2022," nevadaappeal.com.
"Past Pages for August 28 to August 31, 2021," nevadaappeal.com.
"Past Pages for January 1 to 4, 2021," nevadaappeal.com.
"Past Pages for November 3 to 5, 2021," nevadaappeal.com.
"Past Pages for Tuesday, March 15, 2016," nevadaappeal.com.
"Penney to open in Carson," Reno Evening Gazette, p. 17, July 17, 1975.
Penrose, Kelsey. "The History of Nevada Day and its Parade," carsonnow.org, Oct. 28, 2021.
Penrose, Kelsey. "Nevada Lore Series: Brewery Arts Center's history and latest Carson City
    ownership transfer," carsonnow.org, Sept. 9, 2019.
"Peter Vincent 'Cactus Pete' Piersanti," findagrave.com.
Pine Cone Café ad, Reno Evening Gazette, p. 29, May 14, 1964.
"Plan to Display Old V&T Caboose at Carson Goes Awry; Four Cars Loaned Out,"
    Reno Evening Gazette, p. 16, July 21, 1955.
"President Visits Nevada," Los Angeles Evening Express, p. 1, May 19, 1903.
Price, Dave. "Racing community loses a close friend," tahoedailytribune.com, Sept. 18, 2005.
"Prison casino is history," reviewjournal.com, Nov. 26, 2010.
"Prison therapist ordered rehired," The Sacramento Bee, p. B3, March 31, 1995.
" 'Pro' responses still Outnumber 'anti' 3 to 1," Mason Valley News, p. 5, Feb. 20, 1981.
Provost, Stephen H. "America's First Highways," Dragon Crown Books, 2020.
"Railroad Museum Carson City Studied," Nevada State Journal, p. 5, Aug. 5, 1938.
"Remembering Carson's state title basketball team from 40 years ago," nevadaappeal.com,
    Feb. 17, 2015.
"Reno Completes Eventful Year; Here is a Summary of Happenings," Nevada State Journal, p. 1,
    Jan. 2, 1932.
"Reno Forfeits Her Franchise," Reno Evening Gazette, p. 6, July 15, 1907.
"Reno GOP Women Will Visit State Legislature," Reno Evening Gazette, p. 3, Jan. 28, 1963.
"Reno's Nugget Club Gets Gaming Permit," Nevada State Journal, p. 8, Jan. 20, 1954.
"Resort for Carson," Nevada State Journal, p. 3, March 9, 1906.
Rice, Jody. "Historic inn boasts colorful history," Reno Gazette-Journal, p. 1H, Jan. 16, 1999.
Riley, Brendan. "Last Film? 'Bull!' growls the Duke," Reno Evening Gazette, p. 7 Jan. 13, 1976.
Robison, Mark. "Did Nevada have no legal brothels before 1971?" rgj.com, Dec. 15, 2012.
Rocha, Guy Louis. "An Outline of Capital Punishment in Nevada," nsla.nevadaculture.org
    (archived).
"Roosevelt After a Trip to Nevada Resumes His Journey Northward," San Francisco Chronicle,
    p. 5, May 20, 1903.
"St. Charles Hotel," carsonpedia.com.
Sanford, Jim. "A Glance at Sports," Mason Valley News, p. 15, July 12, 1974.
Sanford, Jim. "Role Lyon District Attorney Explained," Mason Valley News, p. 1, July 6, 1979.

Schrantz, Scott. "Carson Motor Lodge Then and Now," aroundcarson.com, April 13, 2013.
Schrantz, Scott. "The Carson Opera House Then and Now," aroundcarson.com, May 22, 2006.
Schrantz, Scott. "Champion Speedway Disaster Zone," aroundcarson.com, June 28, 2008.
Schrantz, Scott. "Dug's West Indies Then and Now," aroundcarson.com, July 8, 2018.
Schrantz, Scott. "Frank Murphy House/Adele's Then and Now," aroundcarson.com, May 6, 2019..
Schrantz, Scott. "Frontier Motel Then and Now," aroundcarson.com, June 16, 2013.
Schrantz, Scott. "Ghosts of Carson: Jack's Bar," aroundcarson.com, Feb. 18, 2012.
Schrantz, Scott. "Ghosts of Carson: Super K," aroundcarson.com, June 6, 2012.
Schrantz, Scott. "Ghosts of Carson: Whistle Stop Inn," aroundcarson.com, April 14, 2022.
Schrantz, Scott. "Heidelberg Bar Then and Now," aroundcarson.com, July 15, 2018.
Schrantz, Scott. "Looking Into the Past," aroundcarson.com, June 23, 2009.
Schrantz, Scott. "Minden Auto Camp Then and Now," aroundcarson.com, June 6, 2018.
Schrantz, Scott. "The Origins of Dug's Windjammer," aroundcarson.com, Dec. 27, 2012.
Schrantz, Scott. "Penguin Burger Then and Now," aroundcarson.com, July 5, 2016.
Schrantz, Scott. "Silver City Mall," aroundcarson.com, May 16, 2009.
Schrantz, Scott. "Washington Street Rails Then and Now," aroundcarson.com, March 15, 2007.
"Seek 'Major Disaster' Status For Huge Western Nevada Area," Nevada State Journal, p. 12, Dec. 27, 1955.
"Sewell to Build Carson City Shopping Center," Reno Evening Gazette, p. 11, Dec. 21, 1963.
"Sharkey's Casino," americantowns.com.
"Sharkey's Casino Review," worldcasinodirectory.com.
"The Shootist," imdb.com.
"Skate Trak – Carson City, NV," dead-rinks.weebly.com.
"Skate Trak offers moms and tots some fun and exercise," Reno Gazette-Journal, p. B1, Nov. 1995.
"Small town serves up big night," Reno Gazette-Journal, p. 1B, July 3, 1988.
Smith, John L. "Ormsby House: Even a great location no guarantee of success," cdcgamingreports.com, Aug. 15, 2018.
"Sparks Acquires Newest Business," Nevada State Journal, p. 8, March 24, 1955.
"Sparks, Fallon, Stewart, Virginia City, Fernley in Finals for Basketball Titles," Reno Evening Gazette, p. 6, March 12, 1966.
"Special Train," Carson City Daily Appeal, p. 4, Nov. 24, 1916.
"Sprawling Carson City System 'Working Well,'" Nevada State Journal, p. 17, Aug. 25, 1969.
Stapleton, Susan. "This Carson City Landmark Restaurant Hits the Market," vegas.eater.com, March 6, 2018.
Steele, Patti. "Masayko came late to Grand Old Party," Reno Gazette-Journal, p. 1, Oct. 23, 1996.
Steinauer, Bill. "In Gardnerville, everyone's heard of Sharkey," Reno Gazette-Journal, p. 2C, Feb. 25, 1978.
"Stewart Indian School's Earl Dunn was area's first basketball star," recordcourier.com, April 1, 2020.
"Suit to close 4 sites dismissed," Reno Gazette-Journal, p. 6B, Oct. 2, 1995.
"Tahoe-Carson Speedway Opens Sunday With Arlan Robinson Benefit," Reno Evening Gazette, p. 23, Aug. 19, 1964.
Tennant, Laura. "Moonlight Ranch still for sale," Mason Valley News, sect. 3, p. 1, April 26, 1991.

Thompson, Bonnie. "The Student Body: A History of the Stewart Indian School, 1890-1940," November 2013.
"To Carson," Mason Valley News, p. 2, April 5, 1963.
"To Organize a State League," Reno Evening Gazette, p. 6, May 14, 1907.
Trent, John. "On the fast track," Reno Gazette-Journal, p. 1E, March 29, 1996.
"Tropicana deal change studied," Reno Evening Gazette, p. 5, Sept. 16, 1976.
"Turner Houston Noses Out Robert Tolson in Carson Race for Mayor, 456-400," Nevada State Journal, p. 28, May 4, 1955.
"University to sell land for Ring Road," Reno Evening Gazette, p. 5, July 19, 1971.
"Unwanted Train Is Given Refuge," Reno Evening Gazette, p. 2, June 20, 1955.
"US 395 history," floodgap.com.
'US State Capitals – By Population!" listchallenges.com.
"USS Carson City saw plenty in its 28-year history," nevadaappeal.com, Nov. 19, 2013.
"Vegas, Fallon, Braves, V.C. Win," Reno Evening Gazette, p. 12, March 14, 1966.
"Virginia and Truckee Railroad Shops, Carson City Nevada," historic-structures.com.
"Virginia City Pulls Upset On Stewart," The Sacramento Bee, p. 16, Dec. 31, 1966.
"V&T Land at Carson Purchased for Hotel," Nevada State Journal, p. 3, April 8, 1955.
Voyles, Susan and Myers, Laura. "Bank closes Carson City's Golden Spike," Reno Gazette-Journal, p. 10B, Nov. 14, 1985.
Warejcka, Mary. "Mail takes ride across state, back in time," Reno Gazette-Journal, p. 17, June 20, 1993.
"Warren Engine Co. No 1," carsonpedia.com.
Waters, Rich. "Formality awaits Carson Senators," Reno Evening Gazette, p. 8, March 8, 1975.
West, Francis. "Old Dutch Mill," aroundcarson.com, Oct. 25, 2007.
"Western Nevada College Celebrates 40 Years," wnc.edu.
"What Makes the Stewart Indian School Unique," stewartindianschool.com.
Wies, Barbara. "Adele's Carson City charms," Reno Gazette-Journal, Best Bets, p. 23, Feb. 22-28, 1996.
"Wilbur's Men's Shop Partnership Formed," Nevada State Journal, p. 14, Aug. 19, 1973.
Weostendiek, John. "Wild West 'sex resort' idea is too wild; couple lose jobs," Miami Herald, p. 15, May 7, 1991.
"Wooster, Reno clash tonight," Reno Evening Gazette, p. 16, Feb. 3, 1975.

Also by the author

Historical nonfiction

    Yesterday's Highways
    America's First Highways
    Highways of the South
    The Great American Shopping Experience
    Martinsville Memories
    Fresno Growing Up
    Highway 99: The History of California's Main Street
    Highway 101: The History of El Camino Real
    The Legend of Molly Bolin
    A Whole Different League

Fiction

    The Talismans of Time
    Pathfinder of Destiny
    Nightmare's Eve
    Death's Doorstep
    Memortality
    Paralucidity
    The Only Dragon
    Identity Break
    Feathercap

Praise for other works

"If you have any interest in highways, old diners and motels and such, or 20th century US history, this book is for you. It is without a doubt one of the best highway books ever published."

— Dan R. Young, founder OLD HIGHWAY 101 group, on **Yesterday's Highways**

"Profusely illustrated throughout, **Highway 99** is unreservedly recommended as an essential and core addition to every community and academic library's California History collections."

— California Bookwatch

"... an engaging narrative that pulls the reader into the story and onto the road. ... I highly recommend **Highway 99: The History of California's Main Street**, whether you're a roadside archaeology nut or just someone who enjoys a ripping story peppered with vintage photographs."

— Barbara Gossett, Society for Commercial Archaeology Journal

"The genres in this volume span horror, fantasy, and science-fiction, and each is handled deftly. ... **Nightmare's Eve** should be on your reading list. The stories are at the intersection of nightmare and lucid dreaming, up ahead a signpost ... next stop, your reading pile. Keep the nightlight on."

— R.B. Payne, Cemetery Dance

"As informed and informative as it is entertaining and absorbing, **Fresno Growing Up** is very highly recommended for personal, community, and academic library 20th Century American History collections."
— John Burroughs, Reviewer's Bookwatch

"An essential primer for anyone seeking an entrée into the genre. Provost serves up a smorgasbord of highlights gleaned from his personal memories of and research into the various nooks and crannies of what 'used-to-be' in professional team sports."
— Tim Hanlon, Good Seats Still Available, on **A Whole Different League**

"The complex idea of mixing morality and mortality is a fresh twist on the human condition. ... **Memortality** is one of those books that will incite more questions than it answers. And for fandom, that's a good thing."
— Ricky L. Brown, Amazing Stories

"Punchy and fast paced, **Memortality** reads like a graphic novel. ... (Provost's) style makes the trippy landscapes and mind-bending plot points more believable and adds a thrilling edge to this vivid crossover fantasy."
— Foreword Reviews

"**Memortality** by Stephen Provost is a highly original, thrilling novel unlike anything else out there."
— David McAfee, bestselling author of

STEPHEN H. PROVOST

33 A.D., 61 A.D., and 79 A.D.
"Provost sticks mostly to the classics: vampires, ghosts, aliens, and even dragons. But trekking familiar terrain allows the author to subvert readers' expectations. ... Provost's poetry skillfully displays the same somber themes as the stories. ... Worthy tales that prove external forces are no more terrifying than what's inside people's heads."

— Kirkus Reviews on **Nightmare's Eve**

About the author

Stephen H. Provost is the author of several books on 20th century America, covering topics that range from his hometown to department stores and shopping centers; from pop music and sports icons to the history of our nation's highways. During a 30-year career in journalism, he worked as a managing editor, sports editor, copy desk chief, columnist and reporter at five newspapers. As a novelist, he has written about dragons, mutant superheroes, and things that go bump in the night. A California native, he now lives in Carson City.

Did you enjoy this book?

Recommend it to a friend. And please consider rating it and/or leaving a brief review online at Amazon, Barnes & Noble and Goodreads.